How to Pass the Theory L Test

When you take the Theory Test you will have to answer 35 multiple-choice questions.

This book covers the complete syllabus of the Test. It includes 300 questions with answers giving full explanations and two mock tests at the end containing 35 questions covering the whole syllabus.

Not only will the book give you the best opportunity to prepare yourself for the Theory Test, but the knowledge you have gained will also make your practical driving lessons more effective and enjoyable.

Good luck!

GW00746644

How to Pass the
THEORY
L TEST

The questions in this book are not taken from the official DSA list. However, they do cover the entire syllabus of the Theory Test and are intended to give the reader an understanding of the principles involved in safe driving.

How to Pass the THEORY ⌐L⌐ TEST

Second Edition

**John Miller, Tony Scriven
and Margaret Stacey**

**KOGAN
PAGE**

YOURS TO HAVE AND TO HOLD
BUT NOT TO COPY

First published in 1996
Reprinted 1996 (three times)
This edition published in 1997

Kogan Page Limited
120 Pentonville Road
London N1 9JN

© John Miller, Tony Scriven and Margaret Stacey, 1996, 1997

British Library Cataloguing in Publication Data

A CIP record for this book is available from the British Library.

ISBN 0 7494 2279 3

Typeset by Saxon Graphics Ltd, Derby
Printed in England by Clays Ltd, St Ives plc

Contents

Contents

About the Authors

The authors each have more than 20 years' experience as Approved Driving Instructors specialising in the training of instructors. Margaret Stacey and John Miller are the authors of the hugely successful book, *The Driving Instructor's Handbook* (Kogan Page), which has the official recommendation of the Department of Transport. They are also co-authors, with Tony Scriven, of *Practical Teaching Skills for Driving Instructors* (Kogan Page). Margaret is also the author of *Learn to Drive* and *The Advanced Driver's Handbook* (Kogan Page).

Margaret, John and Tony believe that all new drivers should have a sound knowledge and understanding of the principles involved in safe driving.

Having successfully taught thousands of new drivers, the authors are well aware of the doubts and fears with which learners approach their Driving Test. With this in mind, this book has been written to help you prepare for the Theory Test so that you will have the confidence to pass first time.

While you are studying for your Theory Test, your driving instructor will teach you how to apply the rules and procedures correctly. This, in turn, will help you develop your driving skills more easily and with a greater understanding so that you will be able to approach your driving lessons and practical test with more confidence.

Introduction

Since the introduction of the first Driving Test in 1935, the content of the Test has hardly changed, apart from the addition of the reverse parking exercise.

Road and traffic conditions, however, have dramatically changed since that time. New drivers now have to be much more highly skilled to be able to cope with the fast-moving traffic and complicated road systems that we have today.

The Driving Test is conducted in two parts:

- A Theory Test which you must pass before you can apply for the practical test.
- A Practical Driving Test.

This format ensures that you understand, and can apply, the principles of safe driving. After all, how can you drive properly if you don't know the rules?

This book has been written to help you understand the rules and regulations for driving so that you will be able to answer the questions in the Theory Test easily. This test consists of 35 multiple-choice questions on a variety of subjects. You have to achieve a minimum number of correct answers to pass.

The syllabus for the exam covers a wide variety of subjects and topics including vehicle safety, hazard awareness, accident procedures, first aid, environmental issues and an understanding of the characteristics of larger vehicles. With the introduction of the theory test there is no longer a requirement for examiners to ask Highway Code questions at the end of the practical test. However, you should not assume that the new theory test simply replaces those questions; the range and complexity of the subjects in the new test means that you should spend some time and effort in preparing for the test and in fully understanding the requirements. This can be done by enrolling on a course at school or college, by attending theory classes organised by your instructor and/or by home study using this book and other relevant material as outlined on page 11. What you should *not* do is try to remember the answers 'parrot fashion'. Remember, it is not just a matter of memorising and answering a few questions on the Highway Code!

Since you may start your practical driving lessons before you take the theory test, it is important that you begin learning the rules which apply to all types of road before you drive on them. Doing this will help you to understand how to apply the rules in different situations. You should then be able to answer the questions in the Theory Test much more easily.

This book is designed, not only to give you the knowledge necessary for driving safely, but also to help you understand why you have to do certain things, and how best to apply that knowledge and understanding.

To help you become a safe and responsible driver, it is also important for you to have a basic understanding of how a car works, the main controls of the vehicle and the routine maintenance to keep it in a roadworthy condition.

The format of the Driving Test has been designed to ensure that new drivers are better prepared for a lifetime's driving. You should think about your driving lessons as 'learning a skill for life' and not just about taking the minimum of lessons to get you through the test. Your driving instructor will teach you how to apply your knowledge and understanding when driving on the road.

By learning to understand and anticipate correctly, and by developing safer attitudes towards yourself, your car and all other road users, you will avoid some of the high-risk situations which put so many new drivers into danger and at risk of losing their driving licence.

When you pass your Theory Test, you will be issued with a pass certificate, details of which must be supplied when you apply for your practical test. This certificate is valid for two years and you should take it with you when you attend for your driving test.

Application forms for both parts of the test are normally available from local driving test centres or from driving instructors. Your instructor will be able to give you the best information about when to apply, the current costs and where the tests can be taken. A sample application form together with current details of the location of theory test centres is included at the end of this book.

We wish you luck with your studies for the Theory Test and with your driving lessons and hope you have a safe and enjoyable future on our roads!

John Miller
Tony Scriven
Margaret Stacey
1997

How to use this book

Each section in this book deals with one or more of the subjects covered in the Theory Test. You will find most of the information you need to help you to answer the questions in the following books:

- *The Highway Code* (published by HMSO);
- *The Driving Test* (published by HMSO);
- *The Driving Manual* (published by HMSO);
- *Know Your Traffic Signs* (published by HMSO);
- *The Advanced Driver's Handbook* by Margaret Stacey published by Kogan Page.

As well as the above publications, you should find *Learn to Drive in 10 Easy Stages* useful when you start your practical driving lessons. This book is a companion to the one you are now working on. It is written by Margaret Stacey, published by Kogan Page and recommended by the Motor Schools Association of Great Britain.

Each section of this book has an introduction followed by some questions. Some of the questions may have more than one correct answer. This is designed to make you think a little more about them and to help you understand the procedures better. At the end of each section you will find the answers to the questions, together with explanations and references to where you will find the relevant information.

Tick the answers you think are correct and record your scores in the progress record at the back of the book. Using a pencil will enable you to erase your ticks and give you the opportunity to go through the questions as many times as you wish until you are achieving full marks.

Your instructor will advise you as to which sections to read in relation to what you are currently learning on your practical driving lessons, and should also help you with the other subjects covered in the Theory Test.

If you have difficulty in understanding any of the questions or answers make a note of them and ask your instructor to explain them to you.

The questions in this book cover the entire syllabus of the Theory Test. However, it would be impossible to include all of the questions which you could be asked in the Test. To prepare yourself properly for 'Driving for Life', you should study carefully the full content of all of the books recommended so that you have a full understanding of the principles involved in safe, economic and effective driving.

SECTION·1

To maintain legal status on our roads, there is a system of regulating drivers and vehicles. This is controlled by the Driver and Vehicle Licensing Authority (DVLA) in Swansea.

This section tests your knowledge of the different documents which drivers and owners of vehicles need to have and the rules relating to them.

You need to know about the rules and regulations relating to:

- driver licensing;
- vehicle licensing;
- learner drivers and their supervision.

Before answering the questions in this section, we recommend that you study the following:

- Forms D100 and V100 – these are available at any main Post Office.
- *The Driving Test* – pages: 9, 10, 11, 15, 16 and 17.
- *The Driving Manual* – pages: 239, 240, 243, 245 and 247.
- *The Highway Code* – rules: 26, 34 and 38; pages: 68, 73, 92 and 93.
- Form DL26 – this is the application for a driving test appointment. You should be able to get one from your driving instructor.

If you study the foregoing pages and rule numbers, you should have no difficulty in answering the questions. Remember to use a pencil to tick those answers you think are correct and record your scores in the Progress Section at the back of the book.

Ask your driving instructor to explain if there is anything you do not understand.

⟨○QUESTIONS○⟩

Remember to select only one answer unless indicated otherwise.

1. **Before you can legally drive on the road you must have:**

   (a) Applied for your first provisional driving licence. ❏
   (b) A physical checkup with your doctor to show you are fit ❏
   to drive.
   (c) Passed the Theory Test and applied for your practical. ❏
   (d) Applied for, received and signed your provisional ❏
   driving licence.

2. **When you apply for your driving licence you must declare that you:**

   (a) Can read a number plate at 20.5 metres (67 feet). ❏
   (b) Wear glasses or contact lenses for close reading work. ❏
   (c) Do not need to wear glasses. ❏
   (d) Have had your eyes tested within the past two years. ❏

3. **Unless you are registered as a disabled person, you may apply for your first provisional driving licence to start on:**

   (a) Your eighteenth birthday. ❏
   (b) Your sixteenth birthday. ❏
   (c) The day you pass the Theory Test. ❏
   (d) Your seventeenth birthday. ❏

4. **While you are learning to drive you may get extra practice. Your supervising driver must:**

   (a) Have passed the Driving Test within the past year. ❏
   (b) Be over 25 and hold a full driving licence. ❏
   (c) Be over 21, having held a full driving licence for three ❏
   years.
   (d) Charge you for the practice sessions. ❏

5. **The car you are learning to drive in must:**

   (a) Display red 'L' plates clearly to the front and rear. ❏
   (b) Display a red 'L' plate in the windscreen and in the rear ❏
   window.
   (c) Display green 'L' plates when practising privately. ❏
   (d) Have dual controls fitted. ❏

6. **To qualify for a full driving licence you must:**

   (a) Pass your driving test within one year of receiving your ❑
   provisional licence.
   (b) Pass the theory and practical elements of the Driving Test. ❑
   (c) Pass the theory and practical elements of the Driving ❑
   Test within a five-year period.
   (d) Have had at least 25 practical driving lessons. ❑

7. **The car you are practising driving in:**

   (a) Must be insured for you as a learner driver. ❑
   (b) Need only be insured for its owner and third parties. ❑
   (c) Need not be insured while you are driving it. ❑
   (d) Must have a cover note for every time you drive. ❑

8. **If a car is kept on the road, it must:**

   (a) Display a tax disc in the windscreen and be properly ❑
   insured.
   (b) Have a legal parking disc. ❑
   (c) Display a certificate of roadworthiness. ❑
   (d) Display a tax disc and insurance certificate in the ❑
   windscreen.

9. **A car which has been registered for more than three years must:**

   (a) Be serviced at least once a year. ❑
   (b) Be registered with the Driving Standards Agency. ❑
   (c) Be MOT tested every year. ❑
   (d) Have new tyres and exhaust system fitted. ❑

10. **When you are insuring your car, the minimum legal insurance required is:**

   (a) The car and its owner. ❑
   (b) The registered owner and any other user. ❑
   (c) Road Traffic Only. ❑
   (d) Any other road user. ❑

11. The vehicle's tax disc should be displayed:

(a) In the left hand side of the windscreen. ❏
(b) Anywhere in the windscreen. ❏
(c) In the window of the nearside front door. ❏
(d) In the window of the driver's door. ❏

12. Vehicles being kept or driven on the road must be registered with:

(a) The County Council. ❏
(b) The local police. ❏
(c) Ministry of Transport. ❏
(d) DVLA in Swansea. ❏

13. Your first provisional driving licence entitles you to drive:

(a) Manual and automatic cars. ❏
(b) Cars with manual gear change only. ❏
(c) Any type of vehicle, as long as your supervising driver ❏
    holds a full licence for that type of vehicle.
(d) Cars and minibuses with more than nine seats. ❏

14. The road fund licence is also referred to as the:

(a) Log book. ❏
(b) Tax disc. ❏
(c) MOT Test Certificate. ❏
(d) Insurance cover note. ❏

15. If the road fund licence on your car expires, you may:

(a) Continue using your car for up to 21 days. ❏
(b) Use it indefinitely until you pay the renewal fee. ❏
(c) Not drive your car or keep it on the road. ❏
(d) Park your car on the grass verge until it is re-taxed. ❏

16. Your first provisional driving licence entitles you to drive under proper supervision:

(a) In any country in the European Union. ❏
(b) Anywhere in the world. ❏
(c) In Europe and in the USA. ❏
(d) In the UK and Northern Ireland. ❏

17. If you commit a motoring offence while you are still learning to drive:

(a) Penalty points cannot be entered and your driving licence cannot be endorsed. ❏

(b) No penalty points can be awarded. ❏

(c) Penalty points can be awarded and, if they are, your driving licence will also be endorsed. ❏

(d) You will automatically be banned from driving for life. ❏

18. If you have endorsements on your provisional driving licence:

(a) You will not be able to take your driving test until these have expired. ❏

(b) You may take your driving test when your instructor advises that you are ready. ❏

(c) You should not show the licence to your driving examiner. ❏

(d) You will not be able to exchange your provisional driving licence for a full one, even if you pass the driving test. ❏

19. Your supervising driver must hold:

(a) A full driving licence for the type of vehicle you are learning to drive. ❏

(b) A driving licence with no endorsements. ❏

(c) An ADI Certificate. ❏

(d) A certificate of competence to drive. ❏

20. If your supervising driver does not have an Approved Driving Instructor Certificate or Trainee Licence you:

(a) Can pay whatever fee you think is acceptable. ❏

(b) Can only pay with goods, such as petrol. ❏

(c) Should not make any payment whatsoever. ❏

(d) Should display green 'L' plates. ❏

21. Your full driving licence will remain valid until the day before your:

(a) 60th birthday if you are female. ❏

(b) 65th birthday if you are male. ❏

(c) 70th birthday. ❏

(d) 75th birthday. ❏

22. **When you have passed your Driving Test, you must apply for your full licence:**

   (a) Within ten years. ❏
   (b) Within two years. ❏
   (c) Before your 21st birthday. ❏
   (d) When you have completed your 'Pass-Plus' training. ❏

23. **If you have any medical conditions which may affect your driving, you must inform:**

   (a) The Driver's Medical Unit at the DVLC, Swansea. ❏
   (b) The local police authority. ❏
   (c) The local health authority. ❏
   (d) The local driving examiner. ❏

24. **MOT certificates are required for cars that have been registered for:**

   (a) One year. ❏
   (b) Two years. ❏
   (c) Three years. ❏
   (d) Five years. ❏

25. **Your car is four years old. What documents would you be required to produce if you were stopped by the police?**

   (a) Your driving licence and the tax disc for the car. ❏
   (b) The vehicle registration document and insurance policy. ❏
   (c) The insurance certificate, MOT certificate and your driving licence. ❏
   (d) The MOT certificate and proof of ownership of the vehicle. ❏

26. **To which of the following must you show your driving licence on demand?**

   (a) A third party after an accident. ❏
   (b) A traffic warden. ❏
   (c) A Department of Transport vehicle inspector. ❏
   (d) A uniformed police officer. ❏

27. **A vehicle registration document will include:**
(Select three answers)

(a) The date from which an MOT certificate is required. ❏
(b) The name of the registered keeper. ❏
(c) The make of the vehicle. ❏
(d) The size of the engine. ❏

28. **When you take your practical driving test, you must have with you:**
(Select two answers)

(a) Your insurance details. ❏
(b) Your car's MOT certificate. ❏
(c) Your passport. ❏
(d) Your driving licence. ❏
(e) Your Theory Test pass certificate. ❏

29. **Before driving another person's vehicle, you should ensure that:**
(Select three answers)

(a) You have their permission. ❏
(b) The vehicle is insured for your use. ❏
(c) The owner has third party cover. ❏
(d) The insurance documents are in the vehicle. ❏

30. **If you normally need to wear your glasses for driving but can't find them, you should:**

(a) Drive more slowly. ❏
(b) Keep to quiet roads. ❏
(c) Wait until it is dark, so the lights will help you. ❏
(d) Find a way of getting home other than driving. ❏

⟨∘ANSWERS∘⟩

1. **The correct answer is (d).**

   You must have received and signed your provisional driving licence before you can drive. It is not legal for you to drive if you have only applied for the licence.

   Refer to: Form D100 'What you need to know about driving licences'; *The Driving Test*, page 9; *The Driving Manual*, Section 12, page 239.

2. **The correct answer is (a).**

   You must be able to read a number plate at 20.5 metres (67 feet). If you need to wear glasses or contact lenses to do this, you should always wear them when driving.

   Refer to: Form D1, 'Application for a driving licence'; *The Highway Code*, rule 34; *The Driving Manual*, Section 12, page 240; *The Driving Test*, page 9.

3. **The correct answer is (d).**

   The minimum age at which you may start driving is 17. If you are a registered disabled person, then you may start at the age of 16.

   Refer to: Form D100, 'What you need to know about driving licences'; *The Driving Manual*, Section 12, page 239.

4. **The correct answer is (c).**

   Your supervising driver must be over 21 and have held a full driving licence for at least three years. This is to ensure that the person sitting with you has some experience. Only ADIs may charge for driving instruction.

   Refer to: *The Driving Test*, page 10; *The Driving Manual*, Section 12, page 247; *The Highway Code*, rule 36.

5. **The correct answer is (a).**

   Red 'L' plates must be displayed clearly to the front and rear of the vehicle whether you are on a lesson or practising privately. If they are placed in the windscreen and rear window they will cause obstruction to your vision. It is not a legal requirement for dual controls to be fitted in a car being used for lessons or practice.

   Refer to: *The Driving Test*, page 16; *The Driving Manual*, Section 12, page 247; *Highway Code*, rule 38.

6. **The correct answer is (b).**

    To qualify for a full driving licence you must pass the theory and practical elements of the Driving Test. When you have passed the theory element, you will have to pass the practical within a two-year period.
    Refer to: 'Application for a Driving Test'.

7. **The correct answer is (a).**

    The car you practice in must have insurance cover for your use of it.
    Refer to: *The Highway Code*, page 68; *The Driving Test*, page 10.

8. **The correct answer is (a).**

    Any car kept on the road must display a valid tax disc and be properly insured. Not displaying a tax disc may render the insurance invalid. Not being insured means that if anything happens to the car while it is on the road, you will not be able to claim for damage.

Refer to: *The Highway Code*, page 68; *The Driving Manual*, Section 12, page 243; Form V100, 'Registering and Licensing your motor vehicle'; *The Driving Test*, page 16.

9. The correct answer is (c).

It is a legal requirement for vehicles which have been registered for more than three years to undergo an 'MOT Test' every year. Service requirements will depend on mileage and manufacturers' recommendations. The Driving Standards Agency has nothing to do with the registering of vehicles. The replacement of tyres, exhaust system and other parts will depend on wear and tear.

Refer to: *The Highway Code*, page 68; Form V100, 'Registering and Licensing your motor vehicle'; *The Driving Manual*, Section 12, page 245.

10. The correct answer is (c).

'Road Traffic Only' or 'Third Party' is the minimum legal insurance requirement. This is normally the cheapest type of insurance but it is not the best because it only covers any other party you might injure or whose property you may damage. It does not cover you for personal injury or damage to your vehicle. You should also check when you drive someone else's car – you may only be covered for this 'third party' risk.

Refer to: *The Driving Manual*, Section 12, page 243.

11. The correct answer is (a).

Refer to: Form V100, 'Registering and Licensing your motor vehicle'.

12. The correct answer is (d).

Vehicles being driven on the road must be registered with the DVLA in Swansea. This is the authority which registers and licences vehicles.

Refer to: Form V100, 'Registering and Licensing your motor vehicle'.

13. The correct answer is (a).

You may drive manual or automatic cars on a provisional driving licence.

Refer to: Form D100, 'What you need to know about driving licences'.

14. The correct answer is (b).

The tax disc.

Refer to: Form V100, 'Registering and Licensing your motor vehicle'.

15. The correct answer is (c).

If your car's road fund licence expires, it will be illegal to drive or keep it on a public road. If you do this you may be fined as well as having to pay an additional penalty. You must apply for a new licence within fourteen days, to run from the expiry date of the previous one. In law a current licence must be displayed at all times when the vehicle is on the road. You should not park your car on a grass verge, whether or not it is taxed.

Refer to: Form V100, 'Registering and Licensing your motor vehicle'.

16. The correct answer is (d).

You need a full driving licence for driving in countries other than the UK and Northern Ireland.

Refer to: Form D100, 'What you need to know about driving licences'.

17. The correct answer is (c).

A learner driver is just as responsible in law as a qualified driver.
Refer to: The Introduction in *The Highway Code*.

18. The correct answer is (b).

Having endorsements on your driving licence will not preclude you from taking a driving test unless you accumulate sufficient penalty points which automatically result in a disqualification under the 'totting up' procedure. You are normally required to show your provisional driving licence to your driving examiner. When you have passed both parts of the test, you will be able to change your provisional driving licence for a full one and any penalty points will be transferred onto it.

Refer to: *The Highway Code*, page 73.

19. The correct answer is (a).

Your supervisor need not hold an ADI Certificate or certificate of competence to drive. Having endorsements on their driving licence will not preclude people from supervising learner drivers. However, it is necessary for anyone supervising to hold a full licence for the category of vehicle being driven.
Refer to: *The Driving Test*, page 10; *The Driving Manual*, Section 12, page 247.

20. The correct answer is (c).

Only Approved Driving Instructors may make a charge, whether this be in cash or goods, for driving lessons. Only red 'L' plates should be displayed by learner drivers.
Refer to: *The Driving Test*, page 9.

21. The correct answer is (c).

Refer to: Form D100, 'What you need to know about driving licences'.

22. The correct answer is (b).

Refer to: Form D100, 'What you need to know about driving licences'.

23. The correct answer is (a).

The DVLC is the only authority which deals with the issue of driving licences and can restrict their issue on medical grounds.

24. The correct answer is (c).

An MOT certificate is required for all cars which have been registered for three years or more. However, some vehicles, such as lorries, buses, taxis and ambulances, are required to have an MOT after one year.
Refer to: *The Driving Manual*, Section 12, page 245.

25. The correct answer is (c).

A police officer may ask you to produce an insurance certificate for your vehicle, the MOT certificate and your driving licence.
Refer to: *The Highway Code*, page 70.

26. The correct answer is (d).

Whenever you are going to drive, you should take your driving licence, your certificate of insurance and, if applicable, your vehicle's test certificate (MOT). It is not a good idea, however, to leave these documents in an unattended vehicle.

Refer to: *The Highway Code*, Section 9, page 70 – providing information to the police.

27. The correct answers are (b), (c) and (d).

When you buy a vehicle make sure that you are given the vehicle registration document (log book). Fill in the 'change of ownership' section and send it off to the DVLA at the address given in the document.

Refer to: *The Driving Manual*, Section 12, page 242.

28. The correct answers are (d) and (e).

The examiner will not be able to conduct the test if you do not have a valid, signed driving licence and your Theory Test pass certificate.

Refer to: *The Driving Test*, page 15.

29. The correct answers are (a), (b) and (c).

Driving a vehicle without the owner's permission could invalidate the insurance cover. You must ensure that valid third party insurance covers your use of the vehicle before driving it.

Refer to: *The Highway Code*, Section 1, page 68.

30. The correct answer is (d).

It is illegal to drive unless your eyesight is up to the standard required for the driving test. It is your responsibility to ensure that you continue to meet the legal eyesight requirements throughout your driving career. If you need glasses for driving then you must make sure you wear them.

Refer to: *The Highway Code*, Section 4, page 68.

SECTION·2

SAFETY EQUIPMENT FOR DRIVERS, PASSENGERS AND OTHER ROAD USERS

Modern cars include many design features to make driving as safe as possible for you, your passengers and other road users.

The footbrake, handbrake, mirrors and indicators should be fairly obvious safety features to you. However, there are other items of equipment which you should know and understand about.

As a driver, you are responsible for the safety of your passengers. Front and rear seatbelts must be worn by law. If there are any children under 14 years of age in your car you must ensure that they wear their seatbelts.

Other safety and warning equipment on the car includes:

- *different types of lights:*
  - sidelights
  - headlights
  - brake lights
  - hazard flashers
  - fog lamps
  - high-intensity rear lights
  - reversing lights;
- *rear view mirrors:*
  - interior
  - offside
  - nearside;
- *other equipment including:*
  - head restraints
  - airbags
  - anti-lock braking systems
  - child safety locks
  - warning triangles
  - fire extinguishers
  - first-aid kits;
- *signals:*
  - indicators
  - horn.

When carrying loads, it is your responsibility to ensure that they fall within the permitted load capacity for the vehicle. Make sure that any loads you carry are secure and do not project dangerously from your vehicle.

The questions in this section of the book should help you to understand about the different types of safety equipment, how they should be used and why they are important.

We recommend that you read the following before you start to answer the questions in this section:

- *The Driving Test* – pages: 16, 21 and 78.
- *The Driving Manual* – pages: 17–19, 30, 36, 42–46, 65, 69, 70, 107, 154, 165, 182, 211, 233, 241, 250, 269 and 271.
- *The Highway Code* – rules: 27, 38, 40, 42, 46, 58, 80, 87, 121, 131–5 and 174; pages: 68, 76, 91 and 92.
- *Know Your Traffic Signs* – pages: 7 and 45.
- *Learn to Drive in 10 Easy Stages* – pages: 23 and 149.

You should also study the handbook of the car you will be driving so that you know where all the controls are and what safety equipment it has.

Tick those answers you think are correct in pencil and then record your score in the Progress Section at the back of the book.

QUESTIONS

Remember to select only one answer unless indicated otherwise.

1. Before driving, there are a number of checks that you need to make to ensure that the car is secure and that you can reach all of the controls comfortably. You should check:

   (a) That the handbrake is on and the gear lever is in the neutral position. ❑

   (b) That the seat is adjusted so that you can reach all of the controls comfortably. ❑

   (c) That the mirrors are adjusted correctly and that you have put on your seatbelt. ❑

   (d) All of the above. ❑

2. When driving after dark in an area where there is street lighting, you must use:

   (a) No lights at all. ❑
   (b) Dipped headlights. ❑
   (c) Headlights on main beam. ❑
   (d) Sidelights only. ❑

3. In which of the following circumstances would you use the hazard warning lights:
   (Select two answers)

   (a) When you have broken down at the side of the road. ❑
   (b) When parking on yellow lines in a built-up area. ❑
   (c) When driving in thick fog. ❑
   (d) When all the traffic ahead of you on the motorway is slowing down suddenly. ❑

4. It is useful to carry in your car:

   (a) A book or newspaper, in case you get held up in a traffic jam. ❑

   (b) A first-aid kit, in case you arrive at the scene of an accident. ❑

   (c) A gallon of petrol in a spare water carrier, in case you run out. ❑

   (d) A scented spray, so that the air does not become stale. ❑

5. **When parking uphill on a steep slope, you are advised to:** **(Select two answers)**

   (a) Park closely to the kerb so that your wheels are wedged ❑
   into it.
   (b) Make sure the handbrake is fully on and select a low gear. ❑
   (c) Turn your front wheels away from the kerb. ❑
   (d) Leave the car in gear with the handbrake off. ❑

6. **Which of the following are not exempt from wearing front seatbelts:**

   (a) Drivers who are reversing. ❑
   (b) Holders of a medical exemption certificate. ❑
   (c) Drivers on short trips to the school or local shops. ❑
   (d) Drivers of delivery vans making local calls. ❑

7. **When carrying a young child in your car, where possible you should:**

   (a) Sit the child in the front with the seatbelt on. ❑
   (b) Sit them in the rear, properly restrained. ❑
   (c) Get an adult passenger to carry the child on their lap. ❑
   (d) Not drive over 30 mph. ❑

8. **Head restraints should be adjusted so that:**

   (a) The driver's shoulders can be supported during long ❑
   journeys.
   (b) The driver's head will not be thrown back in an accident. ❑
   (c) They can be removed prior to a reversing manoeuvre. ❑
   (d) Rear-seat passengers can be seen in the driver's mirror. ❑

9. **High-intensity rear lights should be used:**

   (a) As soon as it starts raining. ❑
   (b) Only in falling snow. ❑
   (c) If the following driver is too close. ❑
   (d) When visibility is less than 100 metres. ❑

10. **Anti-lock braking systems will:**

    (a) Only work when the normal braking system fails. ❑
    (b) Prevent all types of skid. ❑
    (c) Help prevent the wheels from locking up. ❑
    (d) Only work in slippery conditions. ❑

11. Drivers' airbags are becoming more and more common. They:

(a) Ensure the driver has a supply of oxygen in an accident. ❑

(b) Help prevent knee and ankle injuries. ❑

(c) Stop the driver being thrown forward onto the wheel. ❑

(d) Keep the front-seat passenger secure in the seat. ❑

12. Fog lights should be used:

(a) As soon as it is dark enough to use the headlights. ❑

(b) In light drizzle when you need to use the wipers. ❑

(c) When driving in the country and there are no street lamps. ❑

(d) In conditions where visibility is less than 100 metres. ❑

13. It is advisable to carry in your car a:

(a) Fire extinguisher. ❑

(b) Spare pair of driving gloves. ❑

(c) Replacement clutch plate. ❑

(d) Spare set of brake pads. ❑

14. There are various ways in which you can tell others what you are doing. Let following drivers know you are slowing down by:

(a) Changing down through the gears. ❑

(b) Checking the mirrors and using your footbrake. ❑

(c) Switching on your hazard flashers. ❑

(d) Giving a signal with your left arm. ❑

15. Driving at night on full beam, a vehicle overtakes you. Should you:

(a) Keep your headlights on full beam to help the other ❑
driver see the road ahead.

(b) Flash your headlights to let the overtaking driver know ❑
when he has cleared your vehicle.

(c) Dip your headlights as he is going past you. ❑

(d) Let him know it's safe to move back in by tooting your ❑
horn.

16. **Because noise levels are much higher on motorways, what other method, apart from the horn, could you use if it is necessary to warn another driver ahead of you:**

   (a) Your hazard warning lights. ❏
   (b) Give alternate left and right signals with your indicators. ❏
   (c) Flash your headlights. ❏
   (d) Wave out of the window. ❏

17. **The interior mirror should be adjusted so that:**

   (a) You can see the left side of your face in it. ❏
   (b) You can see the nearside pavement in it. ❏
   (c) The top and right-hand edges are lined up with the top ❏
   and right-hand edges of the rear window.
   (d) The Driving Examiner will be able to see you move your ❏
   head when you are checking it.

18. **To help drivers see the edge and centre of the road, and where the lanes are divided, there are different coloured studs. These studs are called:**

   (a) Hazard warning lights. ❏
   (b) Cats' eyes. ❏
   (c) Illuminated flare lights. ❏
   (d) Spacer lights. ❏

19. **The two-door car you are driving has seatbelts fitted to the front seats but not the rear. You are carrying one adult passenger, a child who is 15 years old and one who is 7. Who should sit in the front passenger seat?**

   (a) The adult passenger. ❏
   (b) The 7 year old. ❏
   (c) The 15 year old. ❏
   (d) Whoever will be getting out first. ❏

20. **Child safety locks are fitted to cars so that:**

   (a) Children are locked into their seats, unable to move. ❏
   (b) The rear doors cannot be opened from the inside. ❏
   (c) Children cannot be abducted if left unattended. ❏
   (d) Children cannot climb into the front of the car. ❏

21. **Nearside door mirrors are extremely useful when:**
   (Select two answers)

   (a) Carrying out right-hand reverses. ❑
   (b) Driving in lanes of traffic. ❑
   (c) Driving in foggy conditions. ❑
   (d) Turning left at busy junctions. ❑

22. **The horn can be used:**

   (a) To warn another road user of your presence. ❑
   (b) To express anger when another driver inconveniences ❑
   you.
   (c) To attract the attention of a friend. ❑
   (d) To prevent a dog from running into the road. ❑

23. **When driving into an indoor, multi-storey or underground car park, you should use:**

   (a) No lights. ❑
   (b) Sidelights only. ❑
   (c) Dipped headlights. ❑
   (d) Fog lights, if fitted. ❑

24. **Interior mirrors normally have flat glass so that you get a true picture of what is happening in the road behind. Door mirrors are often made of convex glass. This means:**
   (Select three answers)

   (a) You will get a wider field of vision. ❑
   (b) Vehicles behind will appear to be smaller and therefore ❑
   further away than they really are.
   (c) Vehicles behind will appear to be larger and nearer than ❑
   you think they are.
   (d) You will not get a true picture of what is behind. ❑

25. **Because the mirrors do not cover all of the areas around your car, before you move away from the side of the road you should:**

   (a) Readjust them to check on any blind areas. ❑
   (b) Check the blind spots by looking round over your ❑
   shoulders.
   (c) Open your window and give an arm signal. ❑
   (d) Take a second check in the interior mirror. ❑

26. A properly adjusted head restraint will:

(a) Reduce the risk of a neck 'whiplash' injury. ❏
(b) Be likely to make the driver feel sleepy on long trips. ❏
(c) Restrict vision to the rear of the car. ❏
(d) Mean you can drive faster with greater confidence. ❏

27. You see a vehicle with a flashing green light. This means it is a:

(a) Doctor on an emergency call. ❏
(b) Police car on motorway patrol. ❏
(c) Slow-moving vehicle. ❏
(d) Vehicle carrying hazardous chemicals. ❏

28. When should you use dipped headlights during the day?

(a) All of the time to make sure you are seen. ❏
(b) When driving along narrow roads. ❏
(c) In conditions when visibility is poor. ❏
(d) When parking in built-up areas. ❏

29. If your vehicle breaks down on a motorway and you can't get to the hard shoulder, you should first of all:

(a) Switch on the hazard flashers. ❏
(b) Stop a following driver and ask for help. ❏
(c) Try to repair the vehicle immediately. ❏
(d) Place a warning triangle in your lane. ❏

30. All car passengers must wear a seatbelt unless they are:

(a) Under 14. ❏
(b) Sitting in a rear seat. ❏
(c) Under five feet in height. ❏
(d) Exempt for medical reasons. ❏

∘ANSWERS∘

1. **The correct answer is (d).**

   All of these checks are important for the safety of the driver, passengers and other road users.
   Refer to: *The Driving Manual*, Section 2, pages 17–19 and 30.

2. **The correct answer is (b).**

   Lights are not only to help you see better, but also to help others to see you! Dipped headlights will help other road users to see your vehicle earlier.
   Refer to: *The Highway Code*, rules 131 and 132.

3. **The correct answers are (a) and (d).**

   When parking in a built-up area you should be governed by any parking restrictions. If your car is allowed legally to be there, then you should not need hazard warning lights. To use hazard warning lights on the move could be very confusing for other road users. They should only be used in cases of breakdown, accident or on a motorway in the circumstances described in (d).
   Refer to: *The Highway Code*, rule 134.

4. **The correct answer is (b).**

   Even if you become held up in traffic, you should concentrate on what is happening all around you so that you know when the traffic is about to start moving again. Carrying petrol in containers not intended for that purpose is dangerous. Carrying scented sprays has nothing at all to do with safety. However, carrying a first-aid kit would be very useful if you were involved in, or arrived at the scene of, an accident.
   Refer to: *The Driving Manual*, pages 250 and 269; *The Highway Code*, page 76.

5. **The correct answers are (b) and (c).**

    Leaving the wheels wedged against the kerb could damage your tyres. The most effective way of securing your car when parking on a hill is to use the handbrake, leave it in a low gear and turn your front wheels away from the kerb.
    Refer to: *The Driving Manual*, page 102.

6. **The correct answer is (c).**

    Drivers who have a medical exemption certificate and those who drive vans making local deliveries do not have to wear seatbelts. Any driver may remove the seatbelt when reversing. Even if you are only going on a short trip to the shops you must, by law, wear your seatbelt.
    Refer to: The Road Traffic Act 1988, section 14 – see *The Highway Code*, page 68.

7. **The correct answer is (b).**

    Children are safer when properly restrained in the back of the car. They should not sit behind the rear seats in an estate car or hatchback. You should always make sure that child locks are properly engaged. Even at 30 mph serious injuries can be sustained by anyone who is not restrained properly.
    Refer to: *The Highway Code*, rule 42.

8. **The correct answer is (b).**

Head restraints are to provide maximum protection to the driver's head and neck. They are not for leaning back and resting on during any journey. They should not be removed during any manoeuvring exercises – indeed some cannot be removed as they are built into the seat.

Refer to: *The Driving Manual*, Section 12, page 19; *The Driving Test*, page 21.

9. **The correct answer is (d).**

High-intensity rear lights should be used similarly to fog lights, that is when visibility is less than 100 metres. If they are used in the wrong conditions such as light rainfall or if the following driver is too close, they will cause dazzle and could result in the brake lights becoming masked and more difficult to see.

Refer to: *The Highway Code*, rule 133; *The Driving Manual*, Section 10, page 211; *Learn to Drive in 10 Easy Stages*, Stage 8, page 149.

10. **The correct answer is (c).**

An anti-lock braking system (ABS) can help prevent the wheels from locking up. They cut in when harsh use of the normal braking system has caused the wheels to start locking up. They cannot be guaranteed to prevent all types of skid and they can work in any kind of road condition.

Refer to: *The Driving Manual*, Section 4, page 65.

11. **The correct answer is (c).**

Airbags prevent the driver from being thrown forward onto the wheel and are designed to minimise the type of injury this can cause to the chest and abdomen.

Check your vehicle's handbook to see if your car has an airbag.

12. The correct answer is (d).

Fog lights should only be used when visbility is less than 100 metres and in no other circumstances. Used in the wrong conditions fog lights can cause dazzle to other road users, which in turn can lead to distraction and mistakes being made. Be thoughtful with your use of fog lights.

Refer to: *The Highway Code*, rule 133; *The Driving Manual*, Section 10, page 211; *Learn to Drive in 10 Easy Stages*, Stage 8, page 149.

13. The correct answer is (a).

Of the answers given a fire extinguisher would be the most important item to carry in your car in case of fire, either in your own car or someone else's. If you maintain your vehicle in a roadworthy condition you should not need to carry replacement clutch plates or brake pads. Driving gloves do not really help with safety.

Refer to: *The Driving Manual*, page 271.

14. The correct answer is (b).

If you change down through the gears without braking the following driver will have no warning of your slowing down. Your hazard flashers should not be used in normal circumstances for slowing down. Giving a signal with your left arm will serve absolutely no purpose – the following driver would not be able to see the signal. The safest way to tell a following driver that you are slowing down is to put the M–S–M routine into practice. That is, check your mirror and then slow down with your footbrake – this will operate your brake lights and give the following driver plenty of warning.

Refer to: *The Highway Code*, rule 13; *The Driving Manual*, Section 5, page 69.

15. The correct answer is (c).

If you leave your lights on main beam when the overtaking vehicle pulls back in, the driver will be dazzled by them in the interior mirror. How would you feel if the driver behind was dazzling you? You should avoid flashing your lights unnecessarily as this could be misinterpreted by other road users. When driving in traffic your light beam should fall short of the vehicle in front.

Refer to: *The Driving Manual*, Section 11, page 233.

16. The correct answer is (c).

Because of the high level of noise on the motorway, particularly in wet weather, it is unlikely that your horn will be heard. However, you might in some circumstances, need to let someone know you are there. Flashing headlights is not a generally accepted method of signalling because it can easily be misread. However, in this case it would be safer and probably more effective to make an exception to this rule and flash them. When driving on the motorway, watch out for such signals meant for you!

Refer to: *The Driving Manual*, Section 9, page 182.

17. The correct answer is (c).

Lining up the interior mirror with the edges of the rear window will give you as full a view to the rear as is possible. Adjusting it to see the side of your face will restrict what you can see to the rear as will adjusting it to see the nearside pavement. This mirror should be adjusted so that you can check it with the minimum of head movement.

Refer to: *The Driving Manual*, Section 3, pages 42–5; *The Driving Test*, page 21; *Learn to Drive in 10 Easy Stages*, Stage 2, page 23.

18. The correct answer is (b).

The inventor got the idea for this safety feature, which has been in use since 1934, from the way in which cats' eyes glow in the dark.

Refer to: *Know Your Traffic Signs*, pages 7 and 45; *The Highway Code*, rules 87 and 174.

19. The correct answer is (b).

It is the driver's responsibility to ensure that any passengers under 14 years of age wear seatbelts, even if this means that an adult passenger has to sit in a rear seat.

Refer to: *The Highway Code*, rule 40; *The Driving Manual*, Section 12, page 241.

20. The correct answer is (b).

Young children should be carried in the rear of the car. This is why child locks operate on the rear doors and prevent them from being opened from the inside. Children should be secured in seatbelts or other approved restraints, which should prevent them from moving about too much.

Check to see if the cars which you drive have child safety locks.

21. The correct answers are (b) and (d).

It is important to know what is going on all around you, particularly when you are driving in lanes of traffic. If the traffic is moving very slowly there may be a motorcyclist riding in between the lanes of traffic. At busy junctions you should check your nearside mirror before turning left in case a cyclist is riding along on your left.

Refer to: *The Driving Manual*, Section 3; *Learn to Drive in 10 Easy Stages*, Stage 8; *The Highway Code*, rule 121.

22. The correct answer is (a).

You should only use the horn if you think another road user is not aware of your presence. It should be used lightly and certainly not as a rebuke because you think someone else has made a mistake. Using the horn to attract the attention of a friend may startle someone else. Using the horn near a dog, or any other animal, may frighten it into doing the opposite to what you want it to do!

Refer to: *The Highway Code*, rule 80; *The Driving Manual*, Section 2, page 36; Section 5, page 70; Section 8, page 165.

23. The correct answer is (c).

By using dipped headlights other drivers, who are manoeuvring in and out of spaces, will see your vehicle more easily. Headlights also make it easier for pedestrians to identify a moving vehicle.

Refer to: *The Driving Manual*, Section 7, page 154.

24. The correct answers are (a), (b) and (d).

Door mirrors are made of convex glass to give you a wider range or field of vision. You do not get a true picture of what is happening, and vehicles will appear to be smaller and further away than they really are. You will need more care when you are working out how far away following vehicles are. You can do this by comparing what you see in the door mirrors with the true image you see in the interior mirror.

Refer to: *The Driving Manual*, Section 3, page 43.

25. The correct answer is (b).

Readjusting the mirrors before moving away means that they will not be lined up properly for checking when you are driving along. Giving an arm signal for moving off will not help if someone is already in the blind area. Taking a second look in the interior mirror will still not tell you whether anyone is in the blind area. The safe procedure is to make a final check over your shoulders so that you are sure no other road users are in any of the blind areas.

Refer to: *The Driving Manual*, Section 3, page 46; *The Highway Code*, rule 46; *Learn to Drive in 10 Easy Stages*, page 37.

26. The correct answer is (a).

In the event of an accident, particularly a rear end collision, correctly adjusted head restraints will reduce the risk of head and neck injuries to driver and passengers.

Refer to: *The Driving Manual*, Section 2, page 19; *The Driving Test*, page 21.

27. The correct answer is (a).

Give way to a vehicle displaying a green flashing light as this indicates that it is on the way to an emergency call.

Refer to: *The Driving Manual*, Section 12, page 238.

28. The correct answer is (c).

The purpose of using dipped headlights is to help other road users see your vehicle. Always use them in conditions when visibility is poor.

Refer to: *The Highway Code*, rule 132.

29. The correct answer is (a).

Using your hazard warning lights will alert following drivers to the fact that you have a problem in time to take any necessary action.

Refer to: *The Highway Code*, rule 183.

30. The correct answer is (d).

It is a legal requirement that the driver and all passengers wear a suitable seatbelt or restraint.

Refer to: *The Highway Code*, rule 40.

SECTION·3

There are several different types of road within the UK transport system. Before driving on any of them, you need to know about, and understand, the rules which relate to them so that you will be driving within the law at all times.

As a learner driver, you are not allowed to drive on motorways. However, as soon as you have passed both parts of the driving test you will be allowed to do this immediately, and unsupervised. You must therefore have a good understanding of the rules for driving on the motorway system before you take your test.

You must know how to position correctly on single-laned roads and understand the importance of lane discipline on dual carriageways and motorways.

Different speed limits apply to built-up areas, rural roads and motorways. You must be aware of what the speed limits are, why they apply, and how you can tell when you drive from one speed limit zone into another. This way, you will always be able to keep within the law.

The road signing system has been developed to keep order on the roads and to give yourself and other road users information about:

- what to expect ahead;
- where to position your vehicle;
- parking and waiting restrictions;
- what speed limits apply;
- which directions to take; etc.

To be a safe driver, and to stay within the law, you have to understand what the different road signs and markings mean and how you should respond to them.

Whatever type of road you are driving on, there is a basic routine for you to follow. This is the 'Mirror–Signal–Manoeuvre' routine. It is vital that you understand what this system of driving means and why you should always apply the M–S–M procedure whatever type of hazard you are approaching or manoeuvre you are undertaking. Your instructor will explain this routine to you in the very early stages of your practical driving lessons and you will find that you will be applying it to every task which you carry out on the road.

This section will test your knowledge of the rules and regulations. It should also help you understand where to look for signs and how to respond to them. This information will help when you start your practical driving lessons.

Read the following before starting to answer the questions:

- *The Driving Test* – page: 30.
- *The Driving Manual* – pages: 68, 69, 79, 82, 115, 181, 185, 190, 195, 300–3, 306, 307 and 309.
- *The Highway Code* – rules: 43, 45, 51, 53, 54, 56, 58, 61, 62, 71, 74, 83, 85, 89, 96, 107, 138, 158, 165, 166, 172 and 185; page 80, numbers 4, 5 and 6.
- *Know Your Traffic Signs* – pages: 11, 17, 21, 38, 43, 44, 47, 53, 56, 59, 82 and 85.
- *Learn to Drive in 10 Easy Stages* – pages: 27, 56 and 134.

Remember, if there are any rules, signs or markings you don't understand, ask your instructor to explain exactly what they mean, and how you should deal with them.

Tick the answers you think are correct with a pencil and record your score in the Progress Section at the back of the book.

Remember to select only one answer unless indicated otherwise.

1. **Signs giving orders are normally:**

   (a) Rectangular.　　　　　　　　　　　　　　❑
   (b) Circular.　　　　　　　　　　　　　　　　❑
   (c) Square.　　　　　　　　　　　　　　　　　❑
   (d) Triangular.　　　　　　　　　　　　　　　❑

2. **Driving into a town, you pass a round white sign in a red circle with 30 in black lettering. This means:**

   (a) There is a minimum speed limit of 30 mph.　　❑
   (b) Parking is restricted to 30 minutes in any hour.　❑
   (c) There is a maximum speed limit of 30 mph.　　❑
   (d) It is safe to travel at 30 mph in this area.　　❑

3. **If the white line in the centre of the road becomes longer and the gaps shorter you are:**

   (a) Approaching a single-laned road.　　　　　❑
   (b) Approaching some kind of hazard.　　　　　❑
   (c) Driving into a built-up area.　　　　　　　❑
   (d) Entitled to overtake.　　　　　　　　　　❑

4. **Approaching the end of a road, you notice there is a 'Stop' sign at the junction. You must:**

   (a) Stop your car at the line, apply the handbrake and ☐
   select neutral.
   (b) Stop your car at the line and proceed when you know ☐
   it is safe.
   (c) Keep looking on the approach so that you will know ☐
   whether it is safe to keep moving.
   (d) Only stop if there is traffic behind you. ☐

5. **If you are stopping to give way to pedestrians at a zebra crossing, you should:**

   (a) Wait at the 'Give Way' line. ☐
   (b) Wave them across to encourage them to hurry. ☐
   (c) Flash your headlights to warn oncoming drivers. ☐
   (d) Switch on your hazard flashers to warn following drivers. ☐

6. **If there is a double white line in the centre of the road and the one on your side is broken, you may:**

   (a) Park opposite the line if it is safe to do so. ☐
   (b) Cross the line only if it is safe to do so. ☐
   (c) Overtake any vehicle as long as you do not have to ☐
   cross the line.
   (d) Drive as closely to the line as you can for a better view. ☐

7. The rules relating to urban clearways have been developed to keep the traffic flowing near towns at busy times. You must not stop on an urban clearway:

(a) On Sundays. ❑
(b) At the times stated on the signs. ❑
(c) At lunchtimes. ❑
(d) To set down passengers. ❑

8. Some mini-roundabouts have a white paint marking in the centre of the junction. Should you:

(a) Take the shortest route through the junction. ❑
(b) Only drive over the centre spot if there are no other ❑
road users about.
(c) Try to drive around the centre marking. ❑
(d) Never drive over the centre marking. ❑

9. Traffic lights always follow the same sequence. This is:

(a) Red, Amber, Green, Amber, Green. ❑
(b) Red, Red and Amber, Green, Amber, Red. ❑
(c) Red, Green, Green and Amber, Amber, Red. ❑
(d) Red, Red and Amber, Green, Green and Amber, Red. ❑

10. When the amber light is flashing at a pelican crossing, you should:

(a) Drive on as quickly as possible. ❑
(b) Sound your horn at pedestrians approaching the ❑
crossing.
(c) Stop and wait until the green light appears. ❑
(d) Proceed only if the crossing is clear, checking for ❑
pedestrians who may still cross.

11. If there is a double white line in the centre of the road and the one on your side is continuous, you may:

(a) Never cross the line. ❑
(b) Only park opposite the line if it is safe. ❑
(c) Overtake a cyclist or slow-moving vehicle travelling at ❑
less than 10 mph.
(d) Overtake any vehicle travelling more slowly than you are. ❑

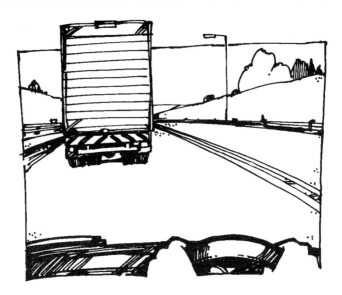

12. When you are learning to drive, by how much must you reduce all of the speed limits which apply to experienced drivers:

(a) By 10 per cent. ☐
(b) By 25 per cent. ☐
(c) By nothing. ☐
(d) By 10 mph. ☐

13. When driving in town, if there were no repeater signs on the lamp-posts, what would be the maximum speed at which you could drive?

(a) 30 miles per hour. ☐
(b) 40 miles per hour. ☐
(c) 25 miles per hour. ☐
(d) 50 miles per hour. ☐

14. When you are driving, you should follow a basic routine for approaching any hazard or junction. This is:

(a) Mirror – Signal – Manoeuvre. ☐
(b) Slow down – Signal – Mirror – Manoeuvre. ☐
(c) Manoeuvre – Signal – Mirror. ☐
(d) Signal – Slow down – Manoeuvre – Mirror. ☐

15. **When driving in lanes, if you wish to get into the next lane on your right, you should:**

    (a) Move over as quickly as possible. ❏

    (b) Move over as slowly as possible. ❏

    (c) Check your mirrors and wait until the last possible ❏
    moment before signalling.

    (d) Check your mirrors, signal if safe and move over ❏
    gradually.

16. **The right-hand lane on a three-lane motorway is for:**

    (a) Cars with a large engine capacity. ❏

    (b) Overtaking only. ❏

    (c) Normal driving if you are driving at the speed limit. ❏

    (d) Cars and coaches only. ❏

17. **If you are driving on a motorway and a red cross is illuminated over your lane, this means:**

    (a) Do not travel any further in this lane. ❏

    (b) You must stop under the light gantry. ❏

    (c) You must leave the motorway via the hard shoulder. ❏

    (d) You cannot travel any further on the motorway. ❏

18. **When joining a motorway, you should use the acceleration lane to:**

    (a) Change up through the gears as quickly as possible. ❏

    (b) Build up your speed to that of the traffic on the main ❏
    carriageway.

    (c) Overtake any other vehicles before joining the main ❏
    carriageway.

    (d) Try to overtake vehicles in the left lane of the main ❏
    carriageway.

19. When leaving a motorway you should:
    (a) Slow down as soon as you reach the countdown markers. ☐
    (b) Get over onto the hard shoulder as soon as possible. ☐
    (c) Signal when you join the deceleration lane. ☐
    (d) Start slowing down as necessary. ☐

20. On a two-lane motorway, the right-hand lane should be used by:

    (a) Cars and coaches only. ❑

    (b) Any vehicle, for overtaking purposes. ❑

    (c) Pedal cyclists and agricultural vehicles only. ❑

    (d) Vehicles travelling at speeds of more than 60 mph. ❑

21. Sometimes minimum speed limits are in force on urban roads. These are to ensure that:

    (a) Traffic is kept moving at a reasonable rate. ❑

    (b) Traffic does not travel at too high a speed. ❑

    (c) Children in the area are protected. ❑

    (d) Traffic does not drive over speed humps too slowly. ❑

22. If you are driving along in a built-up area and are not sure of the speed limit, you should be able to work out if it is higher than 30 mph by:
(Select two answers)

    (a) The speed limit repeater signs. ❑

    (b) The number of houses on at least one side of the road. ❑

    (c) Glancing into side roads to check for speed limit signs. ❑

    (d) A total absence of speed limit signs. ❑

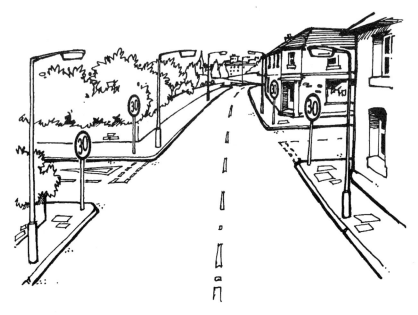

23. Driving out of town, you pass a round white sign with a black diagonal line through it. This means:

(a) The national speed limit applies. ❑

(b) The road has no upper speed limit. ❑

(c) You are on an 'A' road. ❑

(d) The speed limit is 50 mph. ❑

24. Direction signs are normally:

(a) Triangular. ❑

(b) Square. ❑

(c) Rectangular. ❑

(d) Circular. ❑

25. The 'Give Way' sign is the only sign giving an order which is in an inverted triangle. Is this because:

(a) It makes it more recognisable and you will know you are approaching the end of a road. ❑

(b) The words 'Give' and 'Way' fit in better with the sign upside down. ❑

(c) It is an information sign. ❑

(d) You must stop at the end of the road. ❑

26. **Approaching a 'speed hump' in a built-up area, you are advised to:**

    (a) Maintain a speed of 30 mph.   ❑
    (b) Check both pavements for pedestrians.   ❑
    (c) Slow right down.   ❑
    (d) Grip the wheel more tightly.   ❑

27. **When you see a triangular sign at the side of the road, you should:**

    (a) Slow down and stop.   ❑
    (b) Stop for traffic on the major road.   ❑
    (c) Watch out for pedestrians.   ❑
    (d) Look out for hazards ahead, check your mirrors and   ❑
    adjust your speed.

28. **A circular sign with a blue background gives:**

    (a) A warning.   ❑
    (b) An instruction.   ❑
    (c) Directions.   ❑
    (d) Motorway information.   ❑

29. **A clearway sign means:**

    (a) End of built-up area.   ❑
    (b) National speed limit applies.   ❑
    (c) Waiting restrictions apply.   ❑
    (d) No stopping on the clearway.   ❑

30. **When approaching any type of junction, you should apply the following routine:**

    (a) Mirror – signal – speed – position – decide – look.   ❑
    (b) Mirror – speed – signal – position – look – decide.   ❑
    (c) Mirror – signal – position – speed – look – decide.   ❑
    (d) Mirror – signal – speed – position – look – decide.   ❑

(∘ANSWERS∘)

1. **The correct answer is (b).**

    Signs giving orders are normally round.
    Refer to: *the Highway Code*, page 58; *Know Your Traffic Signs*, page 11; *The Driving Manual*, Section 19, page 300.

2. **The correct answer is (c).**

    Minimum speed limit signs have a blue background and white lettering. Parking and waiting restriction signs are normally rectangular. Because there is a maximum speed limit, it does not mean it will be safe to drive up to that speed. A safe speed will be dictated by road and traffic conditions.
    Refer to: *Know Your Traffic Signs*, page 21; *The Highway Code*, rule 56; *The Driving Manual*, Section 19, page 302.

3. **The correct answer is (b).**

    This is a hazard warning line – you should not overtake when approaching any type of hazard.
    Refer to: *The Driving Manual*, Section 19, page 307; *The Highway Code*, rule 83; *Know Your Traffic Signs*, page 44.

4. **The correct answer is (b).**

    You are required by law to stop your car at the line when you see a 'Stop' sign, even if you can see there is nothing approaching. If the main road is clear, there is no need to apply the handbrake or select neutral.
    Refer to: *The Driving Manual*, Section 19, page 301; *The Highway Code*, rules 44 and 109; *Know Your Traffic Signs*; page 17.

5. **The correct answer is (a).**

    You should never harass pedestrians by waving them onto a crossing – an oncoming driver may not have seen them. Hazard flashers should be used in cases of accident or breakdown, not in these circumstances. Wait patiently at the 'Give Way' line to allow the pedestrians plenty of clearance. If it is really busy, it may be advisable to secure your car with the handbrake.
    Refer to: *The Driving Manual*, Section 5, page 79; *The Highway Code*, rule 71; *Know Your Traffic Signs*, page 85.

6. **The correct answer is (b).**

You may cross a broken line only if it is safe to do so. You should not park opposite any double white lines. If you have to overtake you may not be able to keep inside the line because of the width of the road or the obstruction.

Refer to: *The Highway Code*, rules 83, 85 and 138; *The Driving Manual*, Section 19, page 306.

7. **The correct answer is (b).**

Urban clearways are usually on the approach to large towns and cities where traffic becomes very dense at certain times of the day. In order to avoid more problems stopping is prohibited on these roads to keep them clear at particularly busy times. The times at which stopping is prohibited will be stated on signs – make sure you check before you stop!

Refer to: *Know Your Traffic Signs*, page 38; *The Driving Manual*, Section 19, page 303; *The Highway Code*, rule 138.

8. **The correct answer is (c).**

You must try to pass around the white circle. However, this may not always be possible, for example if you are driving a long vehicle. In this case, try to avoid causing inconvenience or danger to other road users.

Refer to: *The Highway Code*, rule 128; *Know Your Traffic Signs*, page 41; *The Driving Manual*, Section 6, page 139.

9. **The correct answer is (b).**

Traffic lights always follow the same sequence so that drivers will know which light is going to appear next. If you are looking well ahead and anticipating properly, you should be able to work out what you will need to do if the lights change.

Refer to: *Know Your Traffic Signs* page 82; *The Highway Code*, page 54; *The Driving Manual*, Section 19, page 309.

10. The correct answer is (d).

Driving on as quickly as possible when the flashing amber light appears could be dangerous if there are pedestrians still on the crossing or if someone steps onto it at the last moment. You should not sound your horn to harass pedestrians – you have no priority. The rule is that you may proceed if the crossing is clear and you are sure no one else is going to step onto it – you do not have to wait for the green light.

Refer to: *Know Your Traffic Signs*, page 85; *The Highway Code*, rule 74.

11. The correct answer is (c).

There is sometimes no alternative to crossing the line, for example if there is an obstruction in the road, you are turning into or out of property, or if you are ordered to cross it by a police officer or traffic warden. You should not overtake others going more slowly than you are unless it is a cyclist or slow vehicle travelling at less than 10 mph. You should not park opposite this line as it will force other road users to cross it.

Refer to: *Know Your Traffic Signs*, page 43.

12. The correct answer is (c).

No discrimination is made between learners and experienced drivers. No matter what your level of experience, the same speed limits apply to all drivers and the type of vehicle being driven.

Refer to: *The Highway Code*, page 53.

13. The correct answer is (a).

In built-up areas there will normally only be repeater signs if the speed limit is higher than 30 mph. Street lights usually indicate that there is a 30 mph limit in force. Remember, however, that the maximum speed at which you can drive safely will also be dictated by the road and traffic conditions.

Refer to: *The Highway Code*, rule 54; *The Driving Manual*, Section 19, page 302; *Know Your Traffic Signs*, page 21.

14. The correct answer is (a).

Whatever type of road you are driving on, the routine procedure you should follow is Mirror–Signal–Manoeuvre. Check your mirrors to see what is happening all around and to work out whether your intended actions will be safe; decide whether a signal will be of benefit to any other road user; carry out your manoeuvre.

Refer to: *The Highway Code*, rule 51; *The Driving Manual*, Section 5, pages 68 and 69; *The Driving Test*, page 37; *Learn to Drive in 10 Easy Stages*, Stage 5, page 56.

15. The correct answer is (d).

You should never change lanes quickly as it could affect another road user. Doing it too slowly could put you in danger if other traffic around you is moving at high speed. Waiting until the last possible moment before signalling may not give enough prior warning of your intention. The only safe way to change lanes is to check it is safe all around, signal at the correct time so as not to confuse, and move over gradually.

Refer to: *Learn to Drive in 10 Easy Stages*, Stage 8, page 134; *The Highway Code*, rules 89 and 96; *The Driving Manual*, Section 5, page 82.

16. The correct answer is (b).

The right-hand lane should be used for overtaking only, regardless of how powerful your vehicle is.

Refer to: *The Driving Manual*, Section 9, page 185; *The Highway Code*, rule 165.

17. The correct answer is (a).

You must not go beyond the signal over your lane. There is some kind of hazard ahead. Check all around to see whether it is safe and move over to an adjacent lane. If all lanes have the signal above them, then you must stop in the lane you are in.

Refer to: *The Highway Code*, rule 172; *The Driving Manual*, Section 9, page 195; *Know Your Traffic Signs*, page 56.

18. The correct answer is (b).

The acceleration lane is for building up speed to that of the traffic on the main carriageway. You should not use it for overtaking. Changing up the gears quickly may not be relevant if there is a large volume of traffic on the motorway travelling at less than normal motorway speeds.

Refer to: *The Highway Code*, rule 158; *The Driving Manual*, Section 9, page 181.

19. The correct answer is (d).

Slowing down when you reach the countdown markers will cause problems on the main carriageway and inconvenience other drivers. Unless there is traffic queueing at the entry to the slip road, you should maintain your speed while still on the main carriageway, slowing down as necessary. Leaving a signal until you reach the deceleration lane will not give following drivers time to react to it. The hard shoulder should only be used in emergencies – it is not an extra lane for leaving the motorway.

Refer to: *The Highway Code*, rule 185; *The Driving Manual*, Section 9, page 190.

20. The correct answer is (b).

To avoid traffic hold-ups any vehicle may use the right-hand lane of a two-lane motorway for overtaking purposes.

Refer to: *The Driving Manual*, Section 9, page 185.

21. The correct answer is (a).

On some urban roads and in tunnels, there is a need to keep the traffic flowing at a reasonable rate. Minimum speed limits are enforced in this type of area.
Refer to: *Know Your Traffic Signs*, page 21.

22. The correct answers are (a) and (c).

If the speed limit is higher than 30 mph then repeater signs are normally sited at regular intervals. Check regularly, particularly if there are overhanging restrictions such as trees. Signs are usually used when there is no regular street lighting or when there is an intermediate speed limit higher than 30 mph. You can also check by glancing into side roads. If you see a 30 mph sign, then the road you are on has a higher limit. The number of houses on either side has absolutely no bearing on the speed limit imposed.
Refer to: *Know Your Traffic Signs*, page 21; *The Driving Manual*, Section 6, page 115.

23. The correct answer is (a).

This sign indicates that the national speed limit applies. Single carriageway roads have a maximum speed limit of 60 mph; motorways and dual carriageways have a maximum speed limit of 70 mph – unless there are signs which indicate a lower limit is in force. These limits are for cars and car-derived vans; different limits apply to larger vehicles.
Refer to: *Know Your Traffic Signs*, page 21.

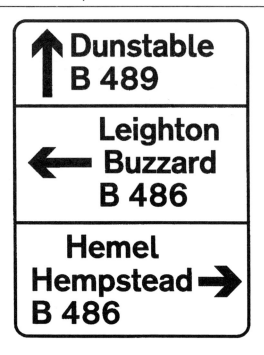

24. The correct answer is (c).

Refer to: *The Highway Code*, page 61; *Know Your Traffic Signs*, page 11.

25. The correct answer is (a).

Both the 'Give Way' and 'Stop' signs are exceptions to the rule of round signs giving orders. This is to make you more aware that you are approaching the end of a road and the other traffic has priority.

Refer to: *Know Your Traffic Signs*, page 17; *The Driving Manual*, Section 19, page 302.

26. The correct answer is (c).

The purpose of speed humps or 'sleeping policemen' is to slow down the traffic in built-up areas where there are more pedestrians around. Driving too fast over the humps could severely damage your vehicle and will make it uncomfortable for your passengers, so use the mirror – signal – manoeuvre routine and SLOW DOWN!

27. The correct answer is (d).

A triangular sign gives warning of a hazard. Use the mirror – signal – manoeuvre routine and adjust your speed accordingly.
Refer to: *The Driving Manual*, Section 19; *The Highway Code*, pages 59 and 60.

28. The correct answer is (b).

Both the colour and the shape of a road sign have certain meanings. You should learn what all the signs mean so that, when you are driving, you can take the necessary action.
Refer to: *The Driving Manual*, Section 19; *The Highway Code*, page 59.

29. The correct answer is (d).

This sign will usually be found on a faster stretch of road when it would be dangerous to stop. Even parking on a grass embankment could restrict the view of following drivers, so park only in the special lay-bys provided.
Refer to: *The Driving Manual*, Section 19; *The Highway Code*, page 58.

30. The correct answer is (c).

The mirror – signal – manoeuvre routine is one of the basic principles of safe driving. The manoeuvre is broken down into position – speed – look. You should only decide on the action to take when you have had time to assess the situation.
Refer to: *The Driving Manual*, Section 8, pages 170 and 171.

SECTION·4

In today's congested traffic conditions, when it seems that the driver behind is pushing you all of the time, it can be extremely difficult to maintain a safe distance between your car and the one in front of you.

You must ask yourself: 'If the driver in front stops suddenly – will I be able to stop too?'

Even in a car with an extremely efficient braking system, you cannot stop your car dead. It will take a few seconds from the moment you realise that you have to brake to the time your car comes to a stop.

The time and distance it takes you to stop your car will depend on:

- your level of concentration;
- your state of health and reactions;
- the efficiency of your brakes;

- the condition of your tyres;
- the type and state of repair of the road surface;
- the weather conditions.

Your life may depend on your understanding of following and stopping distances. You must realise that the higher your speed, the further you will travel before you can stop. On wet roads it will take you even longer – you can at least double the stopping distances when it is raining.

When you are deciding on your following distance from the car in front, you will also have to take into consideration how close the driver behind you is. The closer he or she is, the more distance you will need for stopping in order to give that following driver more time to react.

Your driving instructor will be able to teach you how to judge distances in practice, and how best to use your braking system in the different situations you will find yourself in.

The questions in this section are designed to help you understand about following and stopping distances and why it is important that you not only think for yourself, but also for the following driver.

Read the following before you start working on the questions:

- *The Driving Test* – page: 43.
- *The Driving Manual* – pages: 5, 9, 33, 64, 74, 84, 85, 86, 182, 184, 212, 216–18, 224–7 and 230–3.
- *The Highway Code* – rules: 31, 32, 33, 57, 58, 104 and 161; page 68, 87, numbers 14 and 15 and the table on the back cover.
- *Learn to Drive in 10 Easy Stages* – pages: 52, 127, 150 and 151.
- *The Advanced Driver's Handbook* – pages: 21, 24, 127 and 135.

Remember to select only one answer unless indicated otherwise.

1. The overall stopping distance can be broken down into two separate parts. These are known as:

   (a) The weather and the road conditions. ❑
   (b) The vehicle speed and driver's reaction time. ❑
   (c) The thinking distance and the braking distance. ❑
   (d) Closing speed and braking distance. ❑

2. When stopping, an easy way to estimate your thinking distance is to remember that:

   (a) The thinking distance in feet is about the same as the ❑
   miles per hour you are travelling at.
   (b) Only a fool breaks the two-second rule. ❑
   (c) The faster you are going, the longer it will take you to stop. ❑
   (d) You need to allow at least double the distance on a wet ❑
   or icy road.

3. What is the shortest stopping distance when travelling at 60 miles per hour?

   (a) 12 metres or 40 feet. ❑
   (b) 23 metres or 75 feet. ❑
   (c) 73 metres or 240 feet. ❑
   (d) 96 metres or 315 feet. ❑

4. You should never accelerate when:

   (a) You are going up a steep hill. ❑
   (b) There are solid white lines in the middle of the road. ❑
   (c) Another vehicle is overtaking your car. ❑
   (d) You are travelling in a 30 mph area. ❑

5. When driving on an icy road, you should expect your shortest stopping distance to be:

   (a) Increased by no more than double what it would be on ❑
   a dry road.
   (b) Increased by at least 50 metres. ❑
   (c) Increased by up to ten times as much as it would be on ❑
   a dry road.
   (d) About ten car lengths. ❑

6. **When driving in dry, clear conditions, what would be a reasonable rule to apply to help you estimate a safe separation distance from the vehicle ahead?**

   (a) Allow one foot for every mile per hour of your speed. ❏

   (b) Allow one metre (or yard) for every mile per hour of your speed. ❏

   (c) Stay far enough back so that you can read the number plate of the vehicle in front. ❏

   (d) You should be able to see the wheels of the car in front touching the road – *rubber on road.* ❏

7. **The car behind you is following very closely. Do you:**

   (a) Go a little faster to increase the gap. ❏

   (b) Use the brakes sharply to warn the other driver. ❏

   (c) Make signals to the other driver. ❏

   (d) Ease off gradually and increase the gap between yourself and the car in front. ❏

8. **When carrying out an emergency stop, you should:**

   (a) Brake as hard as possible. ❏

   (b) Push your clutch down first and then brake hard. ❏

   (c) Brake firmly and then push the clutch down if you have time. ❏

   (d) Pull the handbrake up quickly at the same time as braking to help you stop quickly. ❏

9. **If you carry out an emergency stop and the rear wheels skid to the left, you should:**

   (a) Steer to the left to straighten the car. ❏
   (b) Steer to the right to straighten the rear. ❏
   (c) Pull the handbrake up as quickly as possible. ❏
   (d) Move the gear lever into neutral and push down the clutch. ❏

10. **The 'thinking distance' for a driver travelling twice as fast as you are is:**

   (a) The same as your 'thinking distance'. ❏
   (b) 50% more than your 'thinking distance'. ❏
   (c) Twice as much as yours. ❏
   (d) Three times as much as yours. ❏

11. **When driving in dense traffic conditions, you should continually be asking yourself:**
   (Select two answers)

   (a) If the vehicle in front stops, what is it stopping for? ❏
   (b) If the vehicle behind me stops, will I be able to stop? ❏
   (c) Am I too close to the vehicle in front? ❏
   (d) If the vehicle in front stops, will I be able to stop? ❏

12. **The 'braking distance' of a car travelling twice as fast as you are will be:**

   (a) Twice as much as your 'braking distance'. ❏
   (b) Three times as much. ❏
   (c) Four times as much. ❏
   (d) Ten times as much. ❏

13. Your stopping distance depends on:
(Select three answers)

(a) The speed at which you are travelling. ❏
(b) Your reactions. ❏
(c) The weather and state of the road surface. ❏
(d) The condition of the brakes of the car ahead. ❏

14. If you are feeling tired or unwell you will:

(a) Probably be able to stop more quickly. ❏
(b) Probably take longer to react and stop your car. ❏
(c) Need to take stimulants before you drive. ❏
(d) Be able to see further ahead. ❏

15. Driving along on a dual carriageway at 60 mph you can check you are keeping a safe gap by:

(a) Driving at least two seconds behind the vehicle. ❏
(b) Driving at least two minutes behind the vehicle. ❏
(c) Keeping up at the same speed as the vehicle. ❏
(d) Catching up on the vehicle ahead. ❏

16. The greater your speed when you brake:
(Select two answers)

(a) The more difficult it will be to control your car. ❏
(b) The easier it will be to stop. ❏
(c) The further it will take you to stop. ❏
(d) The slower you will need to react. ❏

17. You should always travel at a speed at which:

(a) You can accelerate out of trouble. ❏
(b) You can stop as quickly as possible. ❏
(c) You can use the lowest gear possible. ❏
(d) You can stop within the distance you can see is clear. ❏

18. For the average driver, it takes:

(a) Well over half a second to react. ❏
(b) Well under half a second to react. ❏
(c) At least two seconds to react. ❏
(d) Over one minute to react. ❏

19. When driving at 50 mph in wet conditions allow:
(Select two answers)

(a) About 26 car lengths for stopping. ❏

(b) At least 53 metres (175 feet) for stopping. ❏

(c) At least 106 metres (350 feet) for stopping. ❏

(d) At least 36 metres (120 feet) for stopping. ❏

20. So that space is not wasted in heavy, urban traffic you should:

(a) Always drive as close to the vehicle ahead as possible. ❏

(b) Stay behind at the normal stopping distance for your speed. ❏

(c) Leave at least double the normal stopping distance to allow for following drivers to get in ahead of you. ❏

(d) Keep a gap not less than the thinking distance for your speed. ❏

21. Following and stopping distances on motorways are: (Select three answers)

    (a) The same as those for driving on other roads. ❑

    (b) Reduced to allow for the greater volume of traffic. ❑

    (c) Dictated by the weather and traffic conditions. ❑

    (d) Dictated by the speed at which you are travelling. ❑

22. If you are driving in fog, you should follow at a distance:

    (a) Which allows you to see the rear lights of the vehicle ahead. ❑

    (b) At which you can stop within the distance you can see is clear. ❑

    (c) At which you can read the number plate on the vehicle ahead. ❑

    (d) At which you will have to use the ABS system. ❑

23. Driving closely to the back of a large vehicle:

    (a) Protects you from the effects of side winds. ❑

    (b) Makes the best use of available road space. ❑

    (c) Restricts your vision of the road ahead. ❑

    (d) Allows you to brake earlier for hazards. ❑

24. If you are travelling at 70 mph on a motorway, your thinking distance is:

    (a) Twice that for driving on a normal road. ❑

    (b) Three times that for driving on a normal road. ❑

    (c) About the same as when driving on a normal road. ❑

    (d) Half that for driving on a normal road. ❑

25. **If you are following behind an inexperienced learner driver you should:**

   (a) Overtake as quickly as you can. ❑
   (b) Drive more closely if they are driving very slowly. ❑
   (c) Sound your horn to warn them of your presence. ❑
   (d) Keep well back and allow plenty of time for stopping. ❑

26. **When you are driving in good conditions at 70 mph, what is the shortest stopping distance?**

   (a) 53 metres (175 feet). ❑
   (b) 60 metres (200 feet). ❑
   (c) 73 metres (240 feet). ❑
   (d) 96 metres (315 feet). ❑

27. **When driving at 30 mph in good conditions you need to leave a safe gap between the vehicle in front and your own car. The gap should be at least:**

   (a) Three car lengths. ❑
   (b) Four car lengths. ❑
   (c) Five car lengths. ❑
   (d) Six car lengths. ❑

28. **When driving in freezing conditions you can expect your stopping distance to increase by:**

   (a) Double. ❑
   (b) Three times. ❑
   (c) Five times. ❑
   (d) As much as ten times. ❑

29. **Braking on a wet road, you begin to skid towards the car in front. You are advised to:**

   (a) Brake harder. ❑
   (b) Pull on the handbrake. ❑
   (c) Release the footbrake, then reapply it. ❑
   (d) Steer to the right. ❑

30. **To help avoid running into the car in front, you are advised: (Select two answers)**

   (a) Not to take your eyes off his bumper. ❑

   (b) To watch for brake lights on vehicles further ahead. ❑

   (c) To keep a safe separation distance. ❑

   (d) To brake as hard as you can as soon as you see the brake ❑
      lights of the car in front.

⟨∘ANSWERS∘⟩

1. The correct answer is (c).

When situations arise where you need to slow down, your car will cover some distance while you are thinking about braking. It will travel even further between the moment you apply the brakes up to the time you come to a stop.

It is not enough to memorise the thinking and braking distances shown in *The Highway Code* – your driving instructor should teach you how to judge these distances in practice. In any event, the distances shown are minimum and in bad road conditions you will need to allow more space between you and the vehicle in front.

Refer to: *The Driving Manual*, Section 5, pages 84 and 85; *The Highway Code*, back page.

2. The correct answer is (a).

When travelling at normal speeds, if you are concentrating and reading the road ahead, you will travel approximately the same distance in feet, before you start to brake as the miles per hour at which you are driving. That is, if you are driving at 40 mph, you will travel about 40 feet before you start braking.

Refer to: *The Driving Manual*, Section 5, page 84.

3. The correct answer is (c).

Although learning the stopping distances 'parrot fashion' is a good starting point, it is no good knowing what these are if you cannot 'visualise' the amount of space you need to leave from the vehicle ahead. Instead of thinking in metres or feet, think in terms of how many car lengths you would need to leave for the speed at which you are travelling. Always drive at such a speed that you can stop safely if necessary. Ask your driving instructor to explain the 'two-second' rule to you.

Refer to: *The Highway Code*, rule 57.

4. **The correct answer is (c).**

If you increase your speed while being overtaken, the overtaking driver may be left stranded in the middle of the road with nowhere to go. That person may then be faced with a choice of a head-on collision or having to pull over, forcing you off the road! The most sensible thing to do when being overtaken would be to maintain your speed but be prepared to slow down if the overtaking vehicle is struggling to get past.

Refer to: *The Highway Code*, rule 104.

5. **The correct answer is (c).**

Because all but the most gentle of braking will 'lock' your wheels on packed snow or ice, you should first of all be driving much more slowly than normal. When approaching hazards you will need to be thinking further ahead, braking early and gently, and engaging a lower gear much sooner than usual. When driving in traffic, leave enough distance (as much as ten times more than normal) so that if the car in front gets into difficulty and has to stop, you can also stop safely.

When possible, ask your instructor to arrange a lesson for you in icy conditions, even if this is an 'off-road' session. If you pass the driving test without having driven in bad conditions, don't be frightened to contact your instructor when winter comes along. You will then be able to get some experience and practice safe techniques with an expert by your side. This session could be carried out under the Pass-Plus scheme and count towards some insurance discount for you.

Refer to: *The Driving Manual*, Section 10, pages 216–18.

6. **The correct answer is (b).**

The safety of you and your passengers depends on your being able to accurately judge how far back you should stay. Far too many accidents are caused by 'tailgating' – travelling too close to the vehicle in front. This type of accident quite often involves young or newly qualified drivers and, in most cases, they could be avoided with better judgement and planning. You should allow at least one metre (or yard) for every mile an hour at which you are travelling, between you and the vehicle ahead so that you have plenty of time to react. Ask your instructor to explain this to you.

Refer to: *The Driving Manual*, Section 5, page 86.

7. **The correct answer is (d).**

If someone is following closely behind, not only do you need to allow for your own stopping distance from the vehicle in front, but you also need to allow more space so that you can give the following driver enough time to stop as well. The only way to do this is to increase the distance between your vehicle and the one ahead. This does not necessarily mean driving any slower – it just means that you need to ease back. If you drive faster to get away – the following driver is likely to increase speed to keep up with you, leaving you with even less safety margin. You should not use the brakes sharply in this situation – this could result in the following driver hitting your car. Nor should you use unrecognised signals as a rebuke.

Refer to: *The Driving Manual*, Section 8, page 160.

8. **The correct answer is (c).**

Under normal circumstances you should not pull the handbrake on while the car is on the move. This could cause the wheels to 'lock up' and make things even worse than they are. Braking as hard as possible could result in a skid, and pushing the clutch down first means that you will lose the engine braking and be travelling further than necessary. To keep maximum control brake firmly but progressively. It does not really matter if the engine stalls because you didn't get the clutch down in time – at least the car will stop!

Refer to: *The Driving Manual*, Section 4, page 64.

9. **The correct answer is (a).**

If the rear of the car is going to the left, the front will be going to the right. You therefore need to steer to the left to straighten the front. However, prevention is far better than cure! Emergencies rarely happen if you are looking well ahead and anticipating what might happen. It is much better – and safer – to know how to avoid skidding, than it is to correct it once it has happened.

Refer to: *The Driving Manual*, Section 10, pages 224–7.

10. The correct answer is (c).

'Thinking distance' is based on an average reaction time. Because of this, the distance increases in proportion to the increase in speed. Therefore a driver travelling at twice your speed will take twice as long to 'think' about braking.
Refer to: *The Driving Manual*, page 85.

11. The correct answers are (c) and (d).

It is irrelevant to know why the vehicle ahead is stopping. What is important is that you keep a safe distance from it so that you can stop safely. This should also allow plenty of time for drivers following you to stop as well, particularly if they are close to you. Should the vehicle behind stop, it should not really affect you.
Refer to: *The Driving Manual*, Section 5, page 86.

12. The correct answer is (c).

Braking distances increase significantly as speed is increased. For example, the braking distance at 40 mph is four times that at 20 mph.

13. The correct answers are (a), (b) and (c).

All of these things will affect your stopping distance. The condition of the brakes of another vehicle should not really affect your own performance if you are reacting in good time to what is happening ahead and you are taking into consideration the state of the road conditions. You should in fact be braking before the driver in front by reacting to the brake lights of vehicles further ahead.
Refer to: *The Driving Manual*, Section 5, page 84.

14. The correct answer is (b).

If you are feeling tired or unwell, your attention and reactions will be affected. You will probably not be able to plan far enough ahead and should anything unexpected happen, it will take you longer to react to it. This means that it will also take you longer to stop your car. You should certainly not take stimulants before driving as this is illegal, and anyway they will probably make you become over confident!
Refer to: *The Driving Manual*, Section 1, page 9; Section 5, page 85; *The Highway Code*, rules 31, 32, 33; page 68; *The Advanced Driver's Handbook*, pages 21 and 24.

15. The correct answer is (a).

You should be driving at least two seconds behind the vehicle ahead. Keeping up to the same speed if you are driving too close means that you will not have time to react. You should certainly not be accelerating to get closer to it – this is restricting your thinking and braking time even more. Your instructor will explain about the two-second rule on your practical lessons.

Refer to: *The Driving Manual*, Section 5, page 86; *The Advanced Driver's Handbook*, page 127.

16. The correct answers are (a) and (c).

The greater your speed the quicker you will need to be able to react. Your car will be more difficult to control and it will be harder to stop. The faster you are travelling the further it will take you to stop.

Refer to: *The Driving Manual*, Section 5, page 74.

17. The correct answer is (d).

Accelerating out of one possible danger may take you into another. If you are planning properly you should not have to stop quickly. Using the lowest gear possible is uneconomical as the engine is working harder. You should be able to stop safely well within the distance you can see is clear. This will avoid having to take any last minute sudden decisions to stop.

Refer to: *Your Driving Test*, page 33; *The Highway Code*, rule 57; *Learn to Drive in 10 Easy Stages*, Stage 4, page 52.

18. The correct answer is (a).

The average driver takes well over half a second to react, depending on various factors such as your state of health or whether you are tired or under stress. See also question 14.

Refer to: *The Driving Manual*, Section 5, page 85.

19. The correct answers are (a) and (c).

Remember, in wet conditions you should allow at least double the normal stopping distances.

Refer to: *The Highway Code*, rule 57; 'Shortest Stopping Distances' table on the back page.

20. The correct answer is (d).

It may not be sensible to stay behind at the normal following distance – it could encourage a following driver to overtake you and squeeze in. You should not drive so close to the vehicle ahead that you will not have time to react should it start slowing down. Keep far enough back to allow for a gap not less than your thinking distance, and so that you can at least see where the tyres of the car ahead meet the road.

Refer to: *The Driving Manual*, Section 5, page 86.

21. The correct answers are (a), (c) and (d).

Following and stopping distances are normally dictated by the speed at which a car is being driven. If anything, you should keep more space around yourself when you drive on motorways.

Refer to: *The Advanced Driver's Handbook*, page 135; *The Driving Manual*, Section 9, page 184; *The Highway Code*, rule 161.

22. The correct answer is (b).

If you are following the lights of the vehicle ahead, you may become 'hypnotised' by them and lose your concentration. You will probably be driving too closely to be able to stop – remember you cannot see what is happening beyond that vehicle! You are certainly too close if you can read its number plate. Whatever the conditions, you should drive at a speed so that you can stop within the distance you can see is clear.

Refer to: *Learn to Drive in 10 Easy Stages*, Stage 8, page 151; *The Driving Manual*, Section 10, page 212; *The Highway Code*, rule 58.

23. The correct answer is (c).

Driving too closely restricts your view of the road ahead. You will not be protected from side winds by following too closely as these will be affecting you from the sides. It certainly is not making the safest use of the road space as you will not have enough time to react and brake should the vehicle ahead slow down.

Refer to: *The Advanced Driver's Handbook*, page 127; *The Driving Manual*, Section 8, page 160.

24. The correct answer is (c).

The thinking distance is not affected by the kind of road you are travelling on. If you are alert it is normally the same distance in feet as the miles per hour you are driving at. At 70 mph, therefore, your thinking distance will be about 70 feet.

Refer to: *The Driving Manual*, Section 5, page 85.

25. The correct answer is (d).

No matter what the experience of the driver ahead, you should keep a safe following distance so that you have time to react to whatever they do. You should certainly not drive more closely – this will affect the other driver's concentration and probably worry them into making a mistake. Sounding the horn will have the same effect and should not be used. Be patient, and stay well back until a suitable and safe opportunity to overtake arises.

Refer to: *Learn to Drive in 10 Easy Stages*, Stage 8, page 127; *The Driving Manual*, Section 1, page 5.

26. The correct answer is (d).

Remember that stopping distances increase greatly with wet and slippery roads, poor brakes and tyres, and when the driver is tired.
Refer to: *The Highway Code*, rule 57.

27. The correct answer is (d).

Try to look ahead for brake lights further up the road so that you can anticipate the need to start braking and leave sufficient space so that your braking can be spread over a reasonable distance.

28. The correct answer is (d).

Increase the gap between yourself and the vehicle in front to allow for the extra stopping distance required in these conditions. Plan well ahead and use all of the controls gently and progressively.

29. The correct answer is (c).

Braking too hard can cause the wheels to 'lock up', especially on a wet or icy road surface. When this happens, some drivers instinctively keep their foot pressed on the brake pedal. If the wheels are locked and the car is skidding, the best thing to do is release the brake pedal so that the wheels can regain their grip on the road – then, brake again, but not so hard that you cause another skid.
Refer to: *The Driving Manual*, Section 10, page 227.

30. The correct answers are (b) and (c).

Watching for brake lights further ahead will allow you to anticipate the need for braking. Leaving a safe distance and concentrating on what is happening will reduce the risk of your running into the car in front.
Refer to: *The Highway Code*, rule 57.

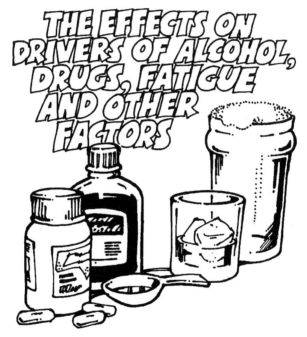

SECTION·5

THE EFFECTS ON DRIVERS OF ALCOHOL, DRUGS, FATIGUE AND OTHER FACTORS

To drive safely you need to be able to concentrate all of the time and respond to what is happening all around you.

To be able to respond properly to the changing circumstances you need to be fit and alert whenever you get into the driving seat.

It is important that you are aware of how different things can affect your concentration. Your driving will be affected if:

- you are feeling tired or unwell;
- your eyesight is not up to standard;
- you are taking drugs of certain kinds;
- you drink alcohol;
- you are thinking about personal problems;
- you have had an argument and are feeling angry;
- you are distracted by music or serious conversation.

The questions in this section are designed to help you understand how any of the above can affect the way in which you drive. Remember, as a driver, you are responsible for the safety of yourself, your passengers and all other road users around you – make sure you are fit before you drive!

Before answering the questions in this section read the following:
- *The Driving Test* – page: 31.
- *The Driving Manual* – pages: 3, 7, 8, 9, 10 and 240.
- *The Highway Code* – rules: 33, 39, 42, 43 and 162; pages 68 and 69.
- *Learn to Drive in 10 Easy Stages* – pages: 16 and 17.
- *The Advanced Driver's Handbook* – pages: 13, 17, 20, 21, 22, 23, 24, 25, 28, 29, 30, 32 and 34.

⟨∘QUESTIONS∘⟩

Remember to select only one answer unless indicated otherwise.

1. **It will take you longer to react to a developing situation if you:**
    - (a) Wear glasses or contact lenses. ❏
    - (b) Are not concentrating on the road. ❏
    - (c) Are feeling fit and healthy. ❏
    - (d) Are driving a car with an ABS system. ❏

2. **If you take medicine bought over the counter without a prescription and then drive your car, it:**
    - (a) Will not affect your driving at all. ❏
    - (b) May make you drowsy and less able to concentrate. ❏
    - (c) Will invalidate your insurance cover. ❏
    - (d) Could invalidate your National Health cover. ❏

3. **If you drive after taking only one small alcoholic drink:**
    - (a) It will not affect your reactions. ❏
    - (b) It will make you much less confident. ❏
    - (c) It could affect your reactions. ❏
    - (d) You are immediately liable to imprisonment. ❏

4. **If you have had an argument with someone you are close to:**
    - (a) You should go for a drive to get it out of your system. ❏
    - (b) Your concentration could be affected. ❏
    - (c) You will have an accident. ❏
    - (d) You should not drive for a minimum of two hours. ❏

5. **If you are taking any prescribed drugs for a minor ailment, you should:**

   (a) Ask your doctor if they will affect your driving. ❏
   (b) Inform the local police. ❏
   (c) Take a rest prior to driving after taking each dose. ❏
   (d) Not take the drugs on the days you will be driving. ❏

6. **If you have to take animals in your car you should:**

   (a) Only let them sit on your lap if they are small. ❏
   (b) Make sure they are restrained and cannot jump around. ❏
   (c) Have a window wide open for them. ❏
   (d) Put them in the boot. ❏

7. **Being over-confident and showing off because you think you are a very good driver could:**
   (Select two answers)

   (a) Result in big improvements in your driving skills. ❏
   (b) Impress your passengers and put them at ease. ❏
   (c) Cause you to drive too fast in the wrong situations. ❏
   (d) Frighten your passengers. ❏

8. **The legal alcohol limit in the UK is:**

   (a) 80 milligrams per 100 millilitres of blood. ❏
   (b) 90 milligrams per 120 millilitres of blood. ❏
   (c) 100 milligrams per 80 millilitres of blood. ❏
   (d) 120 milligrams per 140 millilitres of blood. ❏

9. Drinking a small amount of alcohol before driving:

    (a) May give you a feeling of greater confidence. ❏

    (b) Will improve your driving skills. ❏

    (c) Will improve your popularity as a driver. ❏

    (d) Will speed up your reactions. ❏

10. If you are suffering from a minor complaint such as a cold, your driving:

    (a) Will not be affected. ❏

    (b) Will become illegal. ❏

    (c) May be affected because of a lower level of concentration. ❏

    (d) Will benefit because you will be concentrating more. ❏

11. A lack of fresh air in the car may:

    (a) Cause you to become drowsy. ❏

    (b) Make the windows dirty. ❏

    (c) Affect the heating system. ❏

    (d) Cause exhaust fumes to be drawn in. ❏

12. You will be able to react quickly if:

(a) You have taken pep pills. ❑
(b) You are feeling alert and healthy. ❑
(c) You listen seriously to the radio. ❑
(d) You have noisy passengers in the car. ❑

13. If someone at a party asks you to try some tablets before you drive home, you should:

(a) Not mix them with alcohol. ❑
(b) Take them with plenty of water. ❑
(c) Politely decline the offer. ❑
(d) Phone for a taxi. ❑

14. If your health is liable to affect your ability to drive, either immediately or in the future because of a worsening condition, you should:

(a) Change to a smaller, automatic vehicle. ❑
(b) Notify the DVLA in Swansea. ❑
(c) Only go out driving when you have friends with you. ❑
(d) Only drive during daylight hours. ❑

15. It is not a good idea to drive in the morning if you have had a lot to drink the previous evening because:

(a) You will be sick in the car. ❑
(b) Your breath is likely to offend passengers. ❑
(c) You will need to keep stopping to use the toilet. ❑
(d) You may still be over the alcohol limit legally allowed ❑
   for driving.

16. If you have one arm in plaster, you are advised:

(a) Not to drive until the plaster is removed. ❑
(b) To get your front-seat passenger to change gear for you. ❑
(c) To keep your speed down driving around town. ❑
(d) To fit a steering ball to the wheel. ❑

17. If you suffer a bereavement in the family, this is likely to:

(a) Make you drive a lot faster. ❏
(b) Make you drive a lot more slowly. ❏
(c) Cause you to be more cautious at junctions. ❏
(d) Badly upset your concentration. ❏

18. Whilst on a long journey you start to feel sleepy, but there is nowhere safe to pull over. Do you:

(a) Put your foot down to get to your destination more quickly. ❏
(b) Start counting sheep to keep you awake. ❏
(c) Stop anyway, as you could cause an accident if you continue. ❏
(d) Open the windows and get plenty of fresh air into the car until you find somewhere safe to stop. ❏

19. Having arrived at the firm's Christmas party, you are considering how much you can safely drink before driving home. What choice would you make from the following drinks?

(a) Three pints of beer. ❏
(b) Three spirit drinks. ❏
(c) Three glasses of wine. ❏
(d) Less than any of the above quantities. ❏

20. You have been in a meeting which went on for longer than expected. When you go out to get into your car, thick fog has come down. Because you have arranged for friends to visit you that evening, you decide to brave the elements and go home. You have gone half way and your eyes start to hurt and it becomes difficult to see the road ahead. Do you:

(a) Slow down and check your speedometer from time to time. ❏
(b) Use your wipers to keep the outside of the windscreen clean. ❏
(c) Keep well back from the vehicle ahead. ❏
(d) Do all of the above. ❏

21. Mascots and dolls should:

    (a) Be hung on the driver's mirror. ❑
    (b) Be hung at the top of the rear window. ❑
    (c) Not be placed anywhere in the car where they will restrict ❑
        the driver's view.
    (d) Be hung from the inside light to amuse the children. ❑

22. Listening to a serious programme on the radio may:

    (a) Cause you to lose your concentration. ❑
    (b) Help you to concentrate on what is happening ahead. ❑
    (c) Help to entertain your passengers. ❑
    (d) Cause the battery to run down. ❑

23. Car telephones should be used:

    (a) When they will not affect your control of the car. ❑
    (b) To make personal calls only when you are driving in ❑
        towns.
    (c) To prevent boredom while driving on a motorway. ❑
    (d) Only when the car is stationary. ❑

24. If you have children in the car they should be:
(Select two answers)

(a) Allowed to sit wherever they wish. ❑
(b) Sitting where they have access to a seatbelt. ❑
(c) Kept under control. ❑
(d) Allowed to make as much noise as they wish. ❑

25. The longer your journey, and the further you drive without taking a break:
(Select two answers)

(a) The better your concentration level will become. ❑
(b) The quicker you will be able to react. ❑
(c) The lower your concentration level will become. ❑
(d) You may get drowsy and fall asleep. ❑

26. On a long journey you are advised to stop:

(a) Only when you need petrol. ❑
(b) On the hard shoulder for frequent rests. ❑
(c) When you need to eat. ❑
(d) At least every two hours. ❑

27. To make a long journey more safe, you should: (Select two answers)

(a) Avoid driving on motorways. ❏

(b) Always drive slowly. ❏

(c) Maintain a good supply of fresh air in the car. ❏

(d) Make frequent stops for rest and refreshment. ❏

28. In order to maintain concentration when driving you should:

(a) Not look at passengers when talking to them. ❏

(b) Listen seriously to loud music. ❏

(c) Use a mobile phone to keep alert. ❏

(d) Look at road maps only when in a traffic queue. ❏

29. When driving at night, you are dazzled by oncoming lights. You are advised to:

(a) Close your eyes for a couple of seconds. ❏

(b) Flash your headlights to warn the other driver. ❏

(c) Slow down or stop. ❏

(d) Look away from the light source. ❏

30. If another driver does something that upsets you, you should:

(a) Sound your horn. ❏

(b) Flash your headlights. ❏

(c) Try to overtake the other driver. ❏

(d) Try to stay calm and don't react. ❏

◦ANSWERS ◦

1. **The correct answer is (b).**

   Wearing glasses or contact lenses should not really affect your reaction time. Neither will driving a car with an automatic braking system (ABS). If you are feeling fit and healthy you should be able to react promptly. However, if you lose your concentration your reaction will take much longer should any problem arise. Make sure you keep your attention on what you are doing and on what is happening all around you.
   Refer to: *The Driving Manual*, Section 1, page 3; *The Advanced Driver's Handbook*, page 25.

2. **The correct answer is (b).**

   Many medicines which can be bought without a prescription can cause drowsiness. You must read the directions before you drive. Remember, drowsiness will affect your concentration and probably your reactions too. Taking medicines without a prescription would not normally invalidate your insurance cover and it will have no effect at all on your National Health cover.
   Refer to: *The Advanced Driver's Handbook*, pages 20 and 28; *The Driving Manual*, Section 1, page 9; *The Highway Code*, rule 33.

3. **The correct answer is (c).**

   Alcohol is a drug – taking just one drink could affect your reactions. It could also make you feel over-confident and ready to take risks. You would not normally be liable to imprisonment after one drink. However, if you are going to drive, it is better not to drink at all!
   Refer to: *The Advanced Driver's Handbook*, page 22; *The Highway Code*, rule 39.

4. **The correct answer is (b).**

To go for a drive while you are in a bad mood will most probably affect your concentration. It is also likely to result in your being aggressive towards other road users. This does not necessarily mean that you will have an accident – but it is a possibility! Not driving for a minimum of two hours may be a little unrealistic – however, you should take time to calm down before getting into your car.

Refer to: *Learn to Drive in 10 Easy Stages*, Stage 1, page 16; *The Advanced Driver's Handbook*, page 28; *The Driving Manual*, Section 1, page 3.

5. **The correct answer is (a).**

The most sensible thing to do is ask your doctor if the drugs you are taking will affect your driving. If the answer is 'yes', then you should not drive. Taking a rest before driving will make no difference, the drugs will still be in your system. To stop taking the medication on the days you are driving will not help your condition and anyway the drugs will probably still be in your system. You do not have to inform the police if you are taking prescribed medicines.

Refer to: *The Driving Manual*, Section 1, page 9; *The Advanced Driver's Handbook*, page 24.

6. **The correct answer is (b).**

Animals should be properly restrained when carried in a car. They should not sit on the driver's lap – this is too much of a distraction and, if the animal moves about, could cause the driver to lose control. Having a window wide open might encourage the animal to jump out – this could cause problems for everyone around. It would be cruel to put an animal in the boot of a car without proper ventilation.

Refer to: *The Driving Manual*, Section 1, page 7; *The Advanced Driver's Handbook*, page 30.

7. **The correct answers are (c) and (d).**

   Over-confidence is one of the biggest causes of risk-taking when drivers believe their ability is better than it really is. It is likely to lead you into problems too fast, leaving you with very little space or time to respond. This, in turn, could be a worry to your passengers and other road users around you. It will not do anything for your own confidence either!
   Refer to: *The Driving Manual*, Section 1, page 10; *The Advanced Driver's Handbook*, page 13.

8. **The correct answer is (a).**

   Refer to: *The Highway Code*, page 69.

9. **The correct answer is (a).**

   Drinking may give you a feeling of confidence. However, it will not improve your driving skills. In fact, your skill is likely to deteriorate as you become more likely to take risks. Your reactions will become slower rather than faster. You are unlikely to become more popular if you involve your friends in an accident because you have been drinking!
   Refer to: *The Advanced Driver's Handbook*, pages 22–3; *The Driving Manual*, Section 1, page 9.

10. **The correct answer is (c).**

    Even if you are only suffering from a minor ailment, your concentration level is likely to fall. Although it may not be illegal for you to drive, you will not able to respond as you would if you were fully fit.
    Refer to: *The Driving Manual*, Section 1, page 9; *The Advanced Driver's Handbook*, page 20.

11. The correct answer is (a).

You could become drowsy if the air in the car becomes stale, particularly during a long journey. This will in turn affect your concentration. It is unlikely that stale air will dirty the windows much, unless you only clean your car on rare occasions. It will not affect the heating system nor would it cause exhaust fumes to be drawn into the car.

Refer to: *The Driving Manual*, Section 1, page 8; *The Advanced Driver's Handbook*, page 21.

12. The correct answer is (b).

Your reactions will be at their maximum when you are alert and healthy. They may be affected if you take drugs. Listening seriously to the radio will affect your concentration, which in turn will affect your reactions, as will having noisy passengers in the car.

Refer to: *The Driving Manual*, Section 1, pages 3 and 10; *The Advanced Driver's Handbook*, pages 24 and 25; *Learn to Drive in 10 Easy Stages*, page 17.

13. The correct answer is (c).

The safest option is to decline the offer. Taking unprescribed drugs, particularly in suspicious circumstances, is a recipe for disaster, even if you don't intend driving. Some drugs can make you over-confident to the point of being reckless. If your driving becomes erratic and the police stop you, it could mean the end of your driving career for a while.

Refer to: *The Driving Manual*, Section 12, page 240.

14. The correct answer is (b).

You have a legal obligation to advise DVLA at Swansea if poor health is likely to affect your driving. If you choose to ignore your responsibility and continue driving, you could be putting yourself, your passengers and other road users at risk. Driving in daylight or with accompanying drivers will not make you any safer!

Refer to: *The Driving Manual*, Section 12, page 240.

15. The correct answer is (d).

The other answers are possible. However, if you choose to drive when you know there is a possibility of being over the legal alcohol limit you are taking the risk of, at best, losing your licence, or, at worst, of having a serious accident which could involve innocent people.

Refer to: *The Driving Manual*, Section 1, page 9.

16. The correct answer is (a).

If you cannot control the car properly you should not be driving. As the driver, you are in charge of the vehicle. Driving with one arm out of action would probably restrict your control to the point where you would be driving in a 'careless and inconsiderate' manner. If you were stopped by the police, you could well end up spending the night in prison! This offence carries a penalty of a fine of up to £2500, between 3 and 9 penalty points, and also discretionary disqualification – is it worth the risk?

Refer to: The Penalty Table on page 73 of *The Highway Code*: 'Careless and inconsiderate driving'.

17. The correct answer is (d).

When your mind is elsewhere, your reactions slow down and this could cause danger to yourself, your passengers and other road users. You have already had one death in the family – surely you don't want another one!

Refer to: *The Driving Manual*, Section 1, page 9; *The Advanced Driver's Handbook*, page 17 on emotions.

18. The correct answer is (d).

Driving faster will put you at greater risk if you are tired. Counting sheep is usually a method people use to induce sleep! You should not really stop in a dangerous position so, as a temporary measure, opening the windows wide will produce a flow of air which should freshen you up. However, if you still feel sleepy, you should stop as soon as you reach a safe place. Get out and walk around or, if possible, have a cup of coffee, or take a short nap.

Refer to: *The Driving Manual*, Section 1, page 8; *The Advanced Driver's Handbook*, page 21.

19. The correct answer is (d).

All of the quantities stated are above the legal limit. For some people, especially those not used to drinking, even small amounts of alcohol can have an intoxicating effect. Alcohol reduces co-ordination, increases reaction time, and impairs judgement of speed, distance and risk.

If you are unsure – DO NOT DRINK AND DRIVE!

Refer to: *The Highway Code*, rule 39.

20. The correct answer is (d).

Driving in fog is one of the most dangerous motoring activities. Only travel in fog if you have absolutely no choice. If travel is unavoidable, take the time to check that all of your lights are working and clean, fill your windscreen washer bottle, and clean all of the windows. There is no point in trying to rush to a dinner party if you are taking the risk of not arriving at all!

Refer to: *The Driving Manual*, Section 10, page 210.

21. The correct answer is (c).

Mascots and dolls will not only cause distraction to the driver but, more dangerously, they will restrict vision. They should not be put anywhere in the car where this could happen.

Refer to: *The Driving Manual*, Section 1, page 3; *The Highway Code*, page 68.

22. The correct answer is (a).

Listening to the radio for background music and traffic information can be helpful. However, tuning in to a serious programme may entertain your passengers or keep the children quiet, but it will affect your concentration. You, the driver, are the most important person in the car. If your concentration is affected, then you are putting your passengers at risk. Using the car radio has very little effect on the battery.

Refer to: *The Advanced Driver's Handbook*, page 25; *The Highway Code*, page 68.

23. The correct answer is (d).

You must exercise proper control of your vehicle at all times. You must not use a hand-held microphone unless you are stationary. Even a hands-free unit should not be used if it will distract your attention from driving.

Refer to: *The Highway Code*, rule 43.

24. The correct answers are (b) and (c).

Children under 14 should sit where there are seatbelts and they should be kept under proper control. The choice is not theirs – you are responsible for them! If they become too noisy this will affect your concentration.

Refer to: *The Highway Code*, rule 42.

25. The correct answers are (c) and (d).

The longer you drive, the more tired you are likely to become. This in turn will affect your concentration and reaction times. You may even become so tired that you fall asleep! Plan your journey so that you can take frequent stops, preferably at areas where you can stretch your legs and get refreshments.

Refer to: *The Driving Manual*, Section 1, page 7; *The Advanced Driver's Handbook*, pages 21 and 34; *The Highway Code*, rule 162.

26. The correct answer is (d).

Driving for long distances can be very tiring especially at night, in bad weather conditions, or after a hard day's work. You are advised to stop at least every two hours for a rest, a walk in the fresh air, or to take some refreshment.

27. The correct answers are (c) and (d).

Refer to: *The Driving Manual*, Sections 9, 10 and 11.

28. The correct answer is (a).

You should avoid looking at your passengers while on the move as this can be a distraction. Even at 30 mph your car will travel 45 feet in one second. It is therefore vital that whenever you drive, you concentrate on reading the road well ahead and use all of the mirrors regularly so that you know what is happening all around. Listening to loud music can also be a distraction and using a mobile phone while on the move is illegal.

Reading a map, even if you are in a traffic queue, will also take away your concentration from what is happening on the road. The traffic may start moving and you could be at risk from drivers behind you who may be expecting you to move.

29. The correct answer is (c).

If the headlights of oncoming traffic dazzle you, slow down and, if necessary, stop. Don't look directly into oncoming headlights or be tempted into retaliating if you are dazzled.

Refer to: *The Driving Manual*, Section 11, page 235.

30. The correct answer is (d).

Try not to react to the bad driving habits of others! Take a pride in your own driving and set up a good example to others.

SECTION·6

Learning to handle the car confidently and to apply the rules and regulations relating to driving on different types of road are obviously both very important aspects of learning to drive.

To become a good and safe driver in today's road conditions, it is equally important for you to be aware of everything that is happening around you so that you can act accordingly before the unexpected crops up.

You should be aware that certain types of road user are more at risk than others. These include:

- children;
- the elderly;
- people with prams;

- pedestrians and drivers with disabilities;
- lone women drivers;
- animals.

When you are driving you must concentrate on what you are doing. Scan all around so that you are aware of what is happening and so that you will be able to react to what might happen.

For example, when you see a dog loose on the pavement, expect it to run across the road in front of you. Experienced drivers would be expecting this to happen. However, because of inexperience, new drivers very often don't expect things to go wrong until they actually do and this leaves very little, and often no, time to react.

As a good driver you will need to be able to react, in plenty of time, to what you can see happening, and what might happen.

Another example could be when you are driving along a main road and see a car approaching the end of a road on your left at high speed. You should not assume that the other driver will stop and give way to you. Even if it is your priority, you should be aware that the worst could happen.

Anticipating problems like this in advance means that you will have more time to react safely.

In such circumstances, you should check to see what is happening behind, ease off the gas a little and make sure that the other driver is going to give way to you.

What you may find difficult as a new driver is taking into consideration what you cannot yet see. For example, if you are approaching a bend you should be aware that there could be some sort of traffic hold-up just around the corner. In busy areas, some people push prams out into the road before they have checked it is safe. Children on the way to or from school often jostle each other, with the result that someone could end up in the road in front of you!

When you get out into the country, do not assume that, because you are away from the hustle and bustle of the town, you will have no problems. Think about the combine harvester turning out of a field around the next bend at harvest time, or the cows being herded down the lane at milking time. Look for telltale signs such as straw or manure in the road and anticipate what there might be in the road ahead.

The questions in this section are designed to test your awareness of what you think may constitute a 'hazard'. Once you have passed the practical test and gain experience, you will develop these skills of anticipation. Your instructor can help you with this by taking you into different areas under the Pass-Plus scheme.

In the meantime, you need to understand that you should always 'expect the unexpected'! Before you answer the questions in this section read:

- *The Driving Test* – pages: 30, 34, 40, 41, 42, 44, 45, 46 and 102.
- *The Driving Manual* – pages: 1–4, 7, 10, 68, 71, 77, 78, 79, 82, 88, 89, 95, 118, 119, 120, 122, 142, 158, 165, 166, 168, 169, 173, 174, 175, 176, 177, 181, 186–9 and 309.
- *The Highway Code* – rules: 63, 64, 65, 71, 80, 89, 99, 101, 109, 114, 135, 136, 158, 168 and 177; page: 82, number 16; page: 83, number 21.
- *Learn to Drive in 10 Easy Stages* – page: 64, 67, 140, 141, 142, 144, 145 and 146.
- *The Advanced Driver's Handbook* – pages: 36, 73 and 121.

⟨∘QUESTIONS∘⟩

Remember to select only one answer unless indicated otherwise.

1. The young and elderly are not always able to judge the speed of approaching traffic. They may:
    (Select three answers)

    (a) Step into the road when you do not expect them to. ❏
    (b) Always do the right thing and wait. ❏
    (c) Not see or hear your vehicle. ❏
    (d) Hesitate, even when you are waiting for them. ❏

2. You see a group of young children playing near the edge of the pavement on your left. Another child is on the right side of the road looking across. Should you:

    (a) Brake hard so that you do an emergency stop. ❏
    (b) Keep going at the same speed, but sound your horn. ❏
    (c) Check your mirrors, sound your horn lightly and cover your brake. ❏
    (d) Stop and wave the solitary child across the road. ❏

3. **Driving along a narrow, but straight, country lane you see a horse being ridden on the left verge. There are two cars coming the other way. Would you:**

(a) Keep going at the same speed, tap the horn lightly and give as much clearance as you can. ❏

(b) Check your mirrors, slow down and wait for the two oncoming cars to clear before proceeding slowly past. ❏

(c) Wait for the two oncoming cars, then accelerate past as quickly as possible. ❏

(d) Stay behind the horse until you get to a wider section of road. ❏

4. **You are following a delivery van in a residential area. The van stops suddenly on the left. Should you:**

(a) Check your mirrors, slow down and move out allowing room in case the driver jumps out. ❏

(b) Sound your horn to warn the driver to stay where he is because you are passing. ❏

(c) Accelerate onto the other side of the road to get past quickly. ❏

(d) Stop at the rear of the van until it moves off again. ❏

5. **Driving along in town you see three people chatting on the pavement near a zebra crossing. Should you:**

(a) Assume they are going to stay where they are. ❏

(b) Slow down in case anyone steps out. ❏

(c) Sound your horn loudly to warn them you are near. ❏

(d) Stop at the crossing and wait for someone to cross. ❏

6. **You are turning into a side road on the right which is near the brow of a hill. Would you:**

(a) Turn as early and as quickly as you can in case someone comes over the hill. ❏

(b) Turn in slowly, but before reaching the point of turn, to allow yourself more time. ❏

(c) Sound the horn to warn any oncoming driver you can't see yet. ❏

(d) Make sure you can see properly into the new road before you turn from the normal position. ❏

7. **Driving along a road of normal width, you are catching up with a cyclist who is approaching a parked car on the left. A car coming the other way is almost opposite the parked vehicle. Would you:**

  (a) Check your mirrors and hold back until the oncoming ❑
  car and the cyclist have passed the parked car.
  (b) Sound your horn and expect the cyclist to let you pass. ❑
  (c) Accelerate and try to pass the cyclist before he reaches ❑
  the parked car.
  (d) Slow down to a crawling pace so that you can all get ❑
  through the space at the same time.

8. **An oncoming car is approaching a van parked on its side of the road. Would you:**

  (a) Keep going because it's your right of way. ❑
  (b) Accelerate and try to force the other driver to stop. ❑
  (c) Flash your headlights, move further over to the right ❑
  and keep going.
  (d) Check your mirrors and hold back to see what the other ❑
  driver is going to do before making your decision.

9. **You are approaching traffic lights which have been on green for quite a while. Would you:**

  (a) Check your mirrors and start slowing down in case the ❑
  lights change.
  (b) Accelerate and go through because the amber light allows ❑
  you extra time.
  (c) Change down through all of the gears before stopping ❑
  at the line.
  (d) Flash your headlights to show other drivers you are ❑
  proceeding.

10. Travelling along in the centre lane of a three-lane dual carriageway, you notice that the lorry just ahead in the left lane is catching up on a slower-moving lorry. Would you:

(a) Stay where you are and accelerate to stop the second ☐
lorry from pulling into your lane.

(b) Check your mirrors and, if safe, signal and move over to ☐
the lane to your right to allow the lorry to pull out for overtaking.

(c) Move over to the right-hand lane as quickly as possible ☐
before you become boxed in by anyone behind.

(d) Stay in the centre lane and brake hard to allow the ☐
second lorry to pull out.

11. You are driving at 70 mph in the right-hand lane of a dual carriageway overtaking a slower vehicle. The driver behind flashes his lights warning you that he wishes to overtake. Should you:

(a) Stay where you are so that he can overtake on the left. ☐

(b) Stay where you are because you are not breaking the ☐
speed limit.

(c) Move over quickly to get out of the following driver's way. ☐

(d) Be considerate and move back as soon as you can. ☐

12. One of the most dangerous manoeuvres is overtaking. This is particularly so on single carriageway roads where there may be oncoming traffic. If two vehicles are travelling towards each other at 60 mph on the same course, what would be their 'closing speed'?

(a) 55 miles an hour. ☐

(b) 100 feet per second. ☐

(c) 120 miles an hour. ☐

(d) 200 feet per second. ☐

13. In relation to driving the word 'anticipation' means:

(a) Watching out for all the other idiots on the road. ☐

(b) Taking appropriate action when you think something ☐
will or might happen ahead.

(c) Reading the road ahead. ☐

(d) Expecting all road users to do the correct thing. ☐

14. Anticipation skills can be developed by:

(a) Making early use of the available information. ❑

(b) Making early use of the M–S–M routine. ❑

(c) Attending a classroom course on driving. ❑

(d) Driving as close as possible to the car in front. ❑

15. If you are approaching a car with its reversing lights on and it is being driven into a parking space, should you:

(a) Flash your headlights and sound your horn loudly. ❑

(b) Proceed at the same speed around the other car. ❑

(c) Check your mirrors, slow down and wait to see if the other driver has seen you. ❑

(d) Drive forwards into the parking space because it is convenient for you. ❑

16. You should always be ready to:

(a) Slow down and give way in situations of potential danger. ❑

(b) Accelerate to get through small spaces quickly. ❑

(c) Wave pedestrians across the road. ❑

(d) Show other road users how good a driver you are. ❑

17. **A car is parked on the opposite side of the road. It is your priority but there is a car approaching from the opposite direction at high speed. Would you:**
    (Select two answers)

    (a) Check your mirrors, slow down and be ready to give way. ❑
    (b) Proceed slowly through the gap, sounding your horn. ❑
    (c) Go through the gap as quickly as possible and make the other driver slow down and wait for you. ❑
    (d) Never assume that the other driver will give way. ❑

18. **In the situation below there is a possibility of an accident happening. Which of the drivers do you think would be to blame?**

    (a) The driver of the car parked opposite the junction. ❑
    (b) The driver of the car passing the parked car. ❑
    (c) The driver emerging from the junction. ❑
    (d) All of the three drivers. ❑

19. **In driving the term 'forward planning' means:**
(Select two answers)

   (a) Deciding where you are going to go for your next motoring holiday. ❑
   (b) Looking early so that you can decide how best to approach hazards. ❑
   (c) Reading road signs so that you can decide which lane you need. ❑
   (d) Deciding when you will be able to afford to buy a new car. ❑

20. **In a busy shopping area you should be aware that:**
(Select two answers)

   (a) There are shops on both sides of the road. ❑
   (b) There may be cars parked on both sides of the road. ❑
   (c) Pedestrians may be walking between the parked cars. ❑
   (d) There may be hidden entrances which you cannot see. ❑

21. **Driving along a winding country lane, you see some horse droppings in the road. Would you:**

   (a) Check your mirror, slow down and proceed cautiously around the bend. ❑
   (b) Sound your horn, as there could be a horse around the bend. ❑
   (c) Stop and collect the manure for your garden. ❑
   (d) Wave the following driver past so that they reach the hazard first and will be able to warn you. ❑

22. **You are approaching a motorway and are in the slip road. You should:**
(Select two answers)

   (a) Check to see whether there are any gaps in the left-hand lane of the motorway. ❑
   (b) Drive up to the line, stop and give way. ❑
   (c) Overtake any vehicles which are in the right-hand lane. ❑
   (d) Build up your speed to match that of the traffic in the left-hand lane of the motorway. ❑

23. **You are travelling in town and you see an elderly couple standing in the middle of the road looking in your direction. Would you:**

  (a) Ignore them and keep going because they shouldn't be trying to cross the road in such a dangerous place. ❏

  (b) Check that it is safe, slow down and let them cross out of danger. ❏

  (c) Sound your horn and flash your lights so they will see you. ❏

  (d) Slow right down and wave the pedestrians across the road. ❏

24. **Old people and those with disabilities are very vulnerable. If you saw someone accompanied by a guide dog and carrying a white stick which had two reflective bands around it: (Select two answers)**

  (a) The person is profoundly deaf. ❏

  (b) The person is deaf and blind. ❏

  (c) You should allow the dog to 'guide' the person. ❏

  (d) You should stop and wave them across the road. ❏

25. **When manoeuvring your car you should: (Select two answers)**

  (a) Be aware of the presence of other road users. ❏

  (b) Carry out the exercise as fast as you can. ❏

  (c) Not force others to swerve or slow down. ❏

  (d) Wave them on as soon as you see them approaching. ❏

26. **Driving in a busy shopping street with parked cars on both sides of the road, you should look out for: (Select four answers)**

  (a) Car doors opening. ❏

  (b) Drivers moving off without signalling. ❏

  (c) Vehicles emerging from hidden junctions. ❏

  (d) Special offers in the shop windows. ❏

  (e) Pedestrians stepping out from between parked cars. ❏

27. Cyclists are unpredictable. You should expect them to:
(Select two answers)

(a) Obey the rules of the road. ❏

(b) Ride off the pavement into the road. ❏

(c) Position correctly at junctions. ❏

(d) Wobble about when pedalling uphill. ❏

(e) Look behind before moving around obstructions. ❏

28. You intend turning left at a junction controlled by a 'Stop' sign. There are parked vehicles obscuring your vision into the main road. You should:

(a) Keep moving forwards without stopping until you can see past the obstructions. ❏

(b) Stop at the line, and then proceed cautiously to the left. ❏

(c) Stop behind the line, then creep slowly forward until you can see that it's safe to proceed to the left. ❏

(d) Stop at the line, apply the handbrake, then go when safe. ❏

29. If you are planning a long journey, you should:
(Select two answers)

(a) Organise the trip into reasonable stages. ❏

(b) Drive as far as you can on the first stage. ❏

(c) Drive as fast as you can to reduce the journey time. ❏

(d) Make a note of service areas for taking breaks. ❏

(e) Drive slowly to avoid becoming tired. ❏

30. Approaching a school crossing patrol, you see some older children in the road 50 yards before the crossing. You should:
(Select two answers)

(a) Keep going slowly and sound your horn. ❏

(b) Check your mirrors, slow down and let them cross. ❏

(c) Use your horn to warn them of your presence. ❏

(d) Open the window and tell them to cross at the proper place. ❏

⟨∘ANSWERS∘⟩

1. **The correct answers are (a), (c) and (d).**

   You should not expect any group of road user to always do the right thing! Because of their inability to judge the speed and distance of traffic, young and old people are particularly vulnerable. Because they cannot judge how far away you are – or may not even be aware that you are there – they could step into the road as you are approaching. Even if you make a decision to wait for them, they could hesitate because of their uncertainty. Be patient!

   Young people may sometimes run into the road on purpose – particularly when they are in groups. Be tolerant! If you are looking and planning well ahead, you should be aware of the presence of pedestrians. Try to anticipate their actions, check your mirrors and slow down, just in case. Expect the unexpected!

   Refer to: *The Driving Manual*, Section 8, pages 175 and 176; *The Highway Code*, rules 64 and 65.

2. **The correct answer is (c).**

   Children are unpredictable and easily distracted. They can be totally preoccupied with what they want to do rather than paying attention to the road. If you are planning ahead and have seen the child early enough, there should be no need to brake hard. To keep going at the same speed, even though the horn is sounded, could result in a last minute emergency situation if the child runs out.

   Refer to: *The Highway Code*, rules 63 and 64; *The Driving Manual*, Section 8, pages 165 and 175.

3. **The correct answer is (b).**

   To proceed through at the same time as the oncoming cars would not allow you to give enough clearance to the horse. Using the horn could well frighten the animal and result in a more serious problem. You should not drive past animals quickly as it gives you little time to respond if they react. If you are on a straight country lane and the road ahead is clear, there is no reason why you should not make progress by driving quietly past the horse when it is safe, giving it plenty of clearance.

   Refer to: *The Driving Test*, page 102; *The Highway Code*, rule 80; *The Driving Manual*, Section 8, pages 165 and 175; *Learn to Drive in 10 Easy Stages*, Stage 8, page 147.

4. **The correct answer is (a).**

   You should not assume other drivers will stay where they are when you sound your horn – they could be deaf! Accelerating onto the other side of the road could take you into another hazardous situation. It would not be sensible to stop at the rear of the van – how long is it going to be there, has the driver gone for lunch? The sensible action to take is to make sure it is safe all around and proceed past the van.

   Refer to: *The Highway Code*, rule 136; *The Driving Manual*, Section 5, page 88; Section 8, page 165.

5. **The correct answer is (b).**

   Assuming the pedestrians will stay where they are would result in very little time for you to respond if one steps onto the crossing at the last moment. Sounding the horn loudly could startle them unnecessarily. Pedestrians who are on the crossing have priority – stopping in this particular situation could mean that you are holding up traffic unnecessarily. If you check your mirrors and slow down on the approach, you should be able to pull up safely if a pedestrian steps out. This will also give the following driver plenty of time to stop.

   Refer to: *The Driving Test*, pages 45 and 46; *The Highway Code*, rules 71 and 136; *The Driving Manual*, Section 5, page 79; Section 8, page 165.

6. **The correct answers are (c) and (d).**

   Sounding the horn may well give an oncoming driver warning of your presence. However, turning right as quickly as you can will not give you enough time to check what is happening in the new road. Proceeding before reaching the 'point of turn' or 'cutting the corner' could put a driver approaching the end of the new road into danger. Making sure you can see into the new road means you will know whether there are any obstructions or other problems and turning from the normal position means you will not endanger another road user.

   Refer to: *The Driving Test*, page 42; *The Highway Code*, rule 177; *The Driving Manual*, Section 6, pages 118 and 120; Section 8, page 165; *The Advanced Driver's Handbook*, page 73; *Learn to Drive in 10 Easy Stages*, Stage 5, page 64.

7. **The correct answer is (a).**

   Sounding your horn will probably startle the cyclist and make him wobble around in the road. Accelerating to try to pass before the cycle reaches the car will put you, the cyclist and the oncoming driver into possible danger. Even if you slow down to a crawling speed, you should not try to squeeze through at the same time – cyclists may wobble at any time and you will not have enough room to allow for this.

   Holding back to allow the cyclist and the other car through the gap will mean that you all get through this situation safely and with plenty of spare room.

   Refer to: *The Driving Test*, page 40; *The Highway Code*, rules 99 and 101; *The Driving Manual*, Section 8, pages 165 and 173.

8. **The correct answer is (d).**

   To keep going because you think it's your right of way could result in danger. Never assume that another road user will obey the rules and give way to you. Accelerating to try to force the other driver to stop will result in even more danger. You will, in effect, be narrowing down the road. If the other car does not stop you are now approaching it at a higher speed with less time to react. Flashing your headlights will not help. It may even lead the other driver into thinking you are giving way.

   Holding back to see what the other driver is going to do is the only safe way to approach this situation. Only when you are sure that the other car is continuing or is definitely waiting should you make your decision.

   Refer to: *The Driving Test*, page 41; *The Highway Code*, rule 135; *The Driving Manual*, Section 5, page 88; Section 8, pages 158 and 166.

9. **The correct answer is (a).**

   Accelerating would be unsafe. Amber means proceed only if you cannot stop safely or you have already crossed the line. Changing down through all of the gears is unnecessary – after all the lights may not change. Slow down until you can make a decision to go or stop. If the green light stays on, select the gear appropriate for continuing. If the lights change, stop, apply the handbrake and select neutral. Flashing the headlights in this situation will not help anyone!

You should approach traffic lights at a speed at which you can stop safely if they change. Do not become an 'amber gambler' – someone else approaching from the other direction may be doing the same thing!

Refer to: *The Driving Test*, page 30; *Highway Code*, rule 114; *The Driving Manual*, Section 19, page 309.

10. The correct answer is (b).

Accelerating to stop someone else moving into your lane could lead to danger. If the lorry driver pulls over into your lane when you are accelerating you will have no time to react. If you react by pulling quickly into the right-hand lane without checking to see if it is safe, there could already be someone overtaking you. If you brake hard you could cause problems for following drivers.

Only when you have checked your mirrors, and you are certain it is safe to move over, should you do so. Otherwise you should be anticipating the lorry driver's actions, checking your mirrors and slowing down gradually to allow him space to move over without affecting anyone else.

Refer to: *The Driving Test*, page 44; *The Highway Code*, rules 89 and 168; *The Driving Manual*, Section 5, page 82; Section 9, pages 186–8.

11. The correct answer is (d).

The fact that someone else is breaking the speed limit has nothing to do with you! It might even be an unmarked emergency vehicle travelling to an incident. Even worse, the police may be pursuing that driver. The wisest thing to do would be to move over and let the other driver pass you as soon as it is safe. Avoid panic action or jerky steering as this could cause you to lose control of your vehicle, particularly on a poor road surface.

Think 'defensively' and ask yourself: 'What is the safest course of action?' If you try to stop the other vehicle from passing, the driver may become even more frustrated and get dangerously close to you.

Refer to: *The Driving Manual*, Section 5, page 95.

12. The correct answer is (c).

Before overtaking you should ask yourself: 'Is it safe. Is the vehicle in front going so slowly that I need to get past?' If you think it is necessary, you then ask yourself:

'Is this the right place – shall I do it here?'
'Is this the right time – shall I do it now?'

If you are absolutely sure that overtaking is necessary, and that it will be safe and legal, than get past as quickly as possible. Pull back in leaving enough space so as not to inconvenience or cause risk to any other user.

If in doubt – DO NOT OVERTAKE! Remember, if you are travelling at 60 mph and someone is driving towards you at the same speed, this makes your approach speed 120 mph.

Refer to: *The Driving Manual*, Section 5, page 89.

13. The correct answer is (b).

In any traffic situation, something could happen when you do not expect it. You should always try to 'get the big picture', take everything into consideration – and expect the unexpected. You need to concentrate all of the time and ask yourself questions such as:

'What am I likely to find around this bend?'
'What is that other driver trying to do?'
'Should I speed up or slow down?'
'Will it be safe to keep going, or do I need to stop?'

Refer to: *The Driving Manual*, Section 5, page 68.

14. The correct answer is (a).

Reading the road well ahead and getting the 'big picture' helps. However, anticipation skills go one stage further. Your driving instructor will help you to develop these skills in the early stages of your driving by 'talking you through' potentially difficult situations. When your skill increases, and you begin to make decisions for yourself, your instructor may only occasionally need to prompt you by asking what you should be doing and why. In this way, your anticipation skill should be developed so that you can recognise danger signs early enough to minimise any chance of becoming involved in an accident.

Refer to: *The Driving Manual*, Section 5, page 68.

15. The correct answer is (c).

Reversing lights are warning lights. You should be aware that the other driver may not realise you are there because he is concentrating on the manoeuvre. It would therefore be unsafe to proceed at the same speed. Flashing your headlights or sounding your horn could surprise the other driver and result in a dangerous reaction. Driving quickly forwards into the space would be totally inconsiderate on your part and possibly result in the phenomenon called 'road rage'.

Refer to: *The Driving Manual*, Section 1, page 4 on anticipation; Section 5, page 68 on awareness and anticipation.

16. The correct answer is (a).

No matter who has priority the other driver may be thinking: 'It's my right of way.' Is it worth getting into a potentially dangerous situation to prove you were right? You should never accelerate to race someone through small spaces – what if the other driver decides to do the same thing? You should never wave pedestrians across the road – what if a driver coming the other way hasn't seen them? You should never try to show off and prove how good you are. Everyone is human and we can all make mistakes. What if you make a serious mistake and involve your passengers in an accident? Did you really think this is what they wanted?

Good drivers are responsible, courteous and considerate, keeping any risk to an absolute minimum so that they arrive at their destination safe and relaxed.

Refer to: *The Driving Manual*, Section 1, page 10; *The Advanced Driver's Handbook*, Section 1.

17. The correct answers are (a) and (d).

If you have understood the previous questions you should know that it is not sensible to assume the other driver will always give way. You should therefore check the mirrors, slow down and hold back until you are sure of what is happening. Proceeding through the gap sounding your horn, no matter how slowly you go, will be of little consequence if the oncoming driver also continues. You certainly should not go through the gap at a higher speed and try to force the other driver into submission – no one will win if you meet in the middle!

Refer to: *The Driving Manual*, Section 5, page 88; *The Driving Test*, page 41.

18. The correct answer is (d).

All of the drivers in this situation must take responsibility for some of the blame. The driver of the parked car should not have left it in an illegal and inconsiderate position opposite the junction. This has put all of the other road users at risk. The driver who is passing the parked car has assumed that anyone emerging from the side road will 'give way' because of the road markings, or has not even thought of the possibility of someone emerging. The driver who is emerging from the side road should have checked in both directions and given way to the traffic in the main road. Drivers often only check to the right when they are turning left – watch out for them!

Refer to: *The Advanced Driver's Handbook*, page 36; *The Driving Manual*, Section 8, page 167.

19. The correct answers are (b) and (c).

While you are driving you should be concentrating. Thinking about holidays or new cars will not help you to deal with what is happening around you on the road. Looking well ahead for hazards and changing situations will help you to deal with them when you get there. It avoids any need for last minute braking. Planning also includes reading road signs and markings. The earlier you know whether you will need to change lanes, the easier it will be to get into position without affecting other road users.

Refer to: *The Advanced Driver's Handbook*, Section 3; *The Driving Manual*, Section 5, pages 77 and 78.

119

20. The correct answers are (c) and (d).

The things you can actually see should be quite obvious. That is you can see the shops and cars parked on both sides of the road. What are not so obvious are those things which you can't see! However, in this type of area there will be all sorts of activity hidden from view which you should be expecting.

Your speed should be slow enough that you can react if pedestrians walk out from between the cars. You should be looking out for telltale gaps in the parked traffic – are there entrances there? If you can't see a driver who is about to emerge, can that driver see you?

Refer to: *The Driving Test*, page 41; *The Advanced Driver's Handbook*, page 121.

21. The correct answer is (a).

In this situation (a) is the only safe alternative. If the horse is just around the bend and you sound the horn, you could startle it, putting its rider and anyone else around into danger. Stopping just before a blind bend is dangerous, as is waving the following driver past you. If anyone is coming the other way, you are putting them both at risk.

If you have understood what you have so far learned, you should have been able to work this answer out for yourself!

22. The correct answers are (a) and (d).

You should be planning your approach to the motorway and anticipating what is happening. Looking early for gaps in the traffic in the left-hand lane of the motorway should help you adjust your speed so that you can fit in and keep moving if the situation allows. Driving up to the broken line and deliberately stopping could be dangerous if drivers following you are expecting you to keep moving into a gap which they can see.

If, however, the traffic is dense and travelling slowly on the motorway you may have to give way at the line. If there is a lorry in the right-hand lane of the slip road, you cannot be positive that it is not hiding something travelling along the motorway.

Refer to: *The Highway Code*, rule 158; *The Driving Manual*, Section 9, page 181.

23. The correct answer is (b).

The elderly couple is in a vulnerable positon in the middle of the road. The safest thing to do is check all around and decide whether it is safe to stop and allow them to cross out of danger. If you are looking and planning well ahead, you should have plenty of time to do this. An arm signal to say you are slowing down may help following and oncoming drivers as well as the pedestrians.

You should never wave pedestrians across the road. Another driver may not have seen them! Sounding your horn and flashing your lights in this situation may frighten the couple.

Refer to: *The Driving Manual*, Section 8, page 174.

24. The correct answers are (b) and (c).

If you know that they are deaf as well as blind, you should be aware that you need to take extra care because they won't know you are there! Be careful at pelican crossings – remember they won't see the green flashing man or hear the signal telling them not to start crossing.

If the person has a guide dog, you may also notice an orange band around its collar. Let the dog make the decisions, they are trained to wait until it is safe before crossing. If you stop for them it may cause confusion.

Refer to: *The Highway Code*, rule 64; *The Driving Manual*, Section 8, page 174.

25. The correct answers are (a) and (c).

Wherever you are on the road, and whatever you are doing, you should always be aware of any other road users, including pedestrians, who are around. If you are carrying out any kind of manoeuvre, you should give priority to others. You should not force them to slow down or swerve. Although you should carry out any manoeuvre efficiently, if you try and do it too fast, you will not have time to look properly and might not see someone approaching. You could be inviting someone into danger if you wave them through from one direction and have not checked in the other.

You can only be aware of the presence of others if you are making plenty of observations all around throughout the exercise.

Refer to: *The Driving Manual*, Section 7, page 142; *The Driving Test*, page 34.

26. The correct answers are (a), (b), (c) and (e).

You need to be looking out for all of these problems in busy areas. You should concentrate on what is happening on the road – not in the shop windows.

Refer to *The Driving Test*, page 41; *The Highway Code*, page 82, number 16; *The Driving Manual*, Section 8, pages 168 and 169; *Learn to Drive in 10 Easy Stages*, page 140.

27. The correct answers are (b) and (d).

Because they are so unpredictable, you should not expect cyclists to obey the rules. In windy conditions they are likely to wobble even more.

Refer to: *The Driving Test*, page 40; *The Highway Code*, page 83, number 21; *The Driving Manual*, Section 8, page 173; *Learn to Drive in 10 Easy Stages*, pages 144, 145 and 146.

28. The correct answer is (c).

At a junction controlled by a 'STOP' sign and line you are required to stop behind the line. You must do this and then creep slowly forward until you can see clearly in all directions. Putting on the handbrake may not be necessary because of this need to creep forward until you can see. Only when you are in this position can you make a safe decision to proceed or wait.

Refer to *The Highway Code*, rule 109; *The Driving Manual*, Section 6, page 122; *Learn to Drive in 10 Easy Stages*, page 67.

29. The correct answers are (a) and (d).

Driving as far as you can on the first stage may result in you becoming tired. This will then affect your concentration and safety. Driving as fast as you can will put you at risk – you should always drive at a speed at which you can pull up safely in the distance you can see is clear. Driving too slowly for the conditions can force others into taking risks to get past you. The sensible thing to do is organise your trip into sensible stages, making a note of the places where you can stop to rest.

Refer to: *The Driving Manual*, page 7.

30. The correct answers are (b) and (c).

Children are unpredictable, especially when in groups. Be patient – you should always give pedestrians in the road, no matter where, plenty of time and space. If you think the children may not be aware of your presence, use your horn – but only lightly.

Refer to: *The Highway Code*, rules 63, 64 and 65; *Learn to Drive in 10 Easy Stages*, pages 141 and 142.

SECTION·7

THE CHARACTERISTICS OF DIFFERENT TYPES OF VEHICLE

When you have passed the driving test, your full licence will entitle you to drive larger vehicles as well as cars. You will be entitled to drive vehicles up to 3.5 tonnes as well as minibuses with up to eight passenger seats. These are quite large vehicles compared with the car in which you learnt to drive. You need to recognise and understand that they have different characteristics and have to be driven and responded to accordingly.

Even if you only drive a car, it is necessary for you to understand, and make allowances for, the much larger and heavier vehicles which you meet on the roads.

Goods vehicles and small passenger vehicles often have a restricted view through the rear window and to the nearside because of the load and the lack of windows. This means that you need to be aware of the importance of making all-round observation including using all of the mirrors effectively. You will also need to position your vehicle at junctions so that you have a more effective view of the road and traffic.

You must also make sure that you know the different speed limits which apply when you are driving a small goods vehicle and be aware that your bulkier vehicle will often restrict other drivers' views.

You need to be aware that larger vehicles need more room to manoeuvre. For example, they may need to swing out prior to turning into and out of junctions, and take a different line through roundabouts. They will also take longer to move away and build up speed, particularly when travelling uphill or carrying a full load.

Buses make frequent stopping and moving off manoeuvres and they sometimes do this with very little warning. Other road users can be very easily concealed behind larger vehicles – make sure you can see properly before making any decisions to proceed.

Watch out for cars towing caravans or other trailers. They may take unusual courses through junctions or sway about, especially if it is windy.

Because of their size, cycles and motorcycles are more difficult to see. When you are emerging from junctions make sure the road is clear before you pull out by continually looking in all directions. Remember that motorcycles often approach at quite high speeds and go through small gaps in traffic.

In busy areas, and when you are driving in lanes of traffic, get into the habit of using all of your mirrors so that you know exactly who is there and what is happening all around you.

Before you answer the questions in this section, read:

- *The Driving Manual*, pages: 90, 103, 110, 168, 173, 188, 207, 209, 238, 280 and 281.
- *The Highway Code*, rules: 76–9, 97, 98, 101, 103, 122, 126, 127, 140 and 154.
- *Learn to Drive in 10 Easy Stages* – pages: 136, 137 and 152.
- *The Advanced Driver's Handbook* – pages: 127, 132, 138 and 108.

⦿QUESTIONS⦿

Remember to select only one answer unless indicated otherwise.

1. If you were driving a large or slow-moving vehicle on a narrow winding road and there were other, faster-moving, vehicles following you, what should you do?

   (a) Make a detour to avoid other traffic. ❏
   (b) Keep checking your mirrors to see how the situation develops. ❏
   (c) Pull in where it is safe so that others can pass you. ❏
   (d) Stop immediately and wave them past. ❏

2. You are driving in town and see a stationary bus at a bus stop. Should you:
   (Select three answers)

   (a) Expect the bus to move away without a signal. ❏
   (b) Drive past as quickly as you can. ❏
   (c) Look for passengers walking out in front of the bus. ❏
   (d) Be ready to hold back and give way in case the bus moves off. ❏

3. You are driving behind a large goods vehicle on a road which has recently been resurfaced. You are advised to:

   (a) Keep well back in case loose chippings are thrown up and break your windscreen. ❏
   (b) Get past the lorry as soon as possible. ❏
   (c) Watch out as the lorry is likely to start skidding on the new surface. ❏
   (d) Flash your lights to let the lorry driver know you are there ❏

4. You are following a large goods vehicle approaching a cross-road. The LGV has on its left signal but is moving out towards the middle of the road. Would you:

   (a) Assume that the driver has put on the wrong signal and will be turning right. ❏
   (b) Hang back because the vehicle is likely to be turning left. ❏
   (c) Flash your lights to warn the driver ahead that the indicators are on. ❏
   (d) Check your mirrors, move out and overtake as quickly as you can. ❏

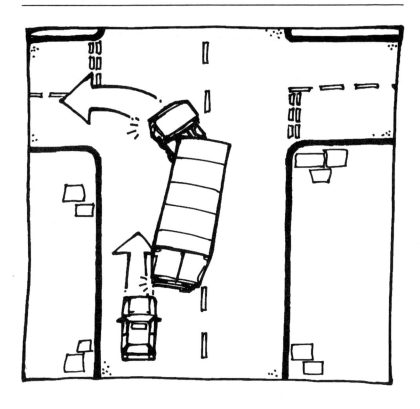

5. **You are waiting to emerge from a narrow side road and you see a large goods vehicle approaching from your right with a left signal flashing. Do you:**

(a) Pull out of the side road to leave room for the lorry. ☐
(b) Wait until the lorry has completed the turn into the side road. ☐
(c) Reverse your car back into the side road away from the junction. ☐
(d) Be ready to move out if necessary, and when safe. ☐

6. **Ideally, the total weight of a trailer should be no more than a certain percentage of the empty weight of the towing vehicle. This percentage is:**

    (a) 70%. ❏
    (b) 75%. ❏
    (c) 85%. ❏
    (d) 90%. ❏

7. **When you are towing a relatively heavy trailer or a caravan, you need to allow more time and distance for overtaking. This time and distance is:**

    (a) Twice as much as normal. ❏
    (b) 50% more than normal. ❏
    (c) 25% more than normal. ❏
    (d) Three times as much. ❏

8. **Trailers (including caravans) should be loaded so that:**

    (a) Any heavier items are placed over the axle. ❏
    (b) Most of the weight is at the front of the trailer. ❏
    (c) Most of the weight is at the back of the trailer. ❏
    (d) Any heavier items are spread along the whole length of ❏
        the trailer.

9. **You are towing a trailer on a motorway. The maximum speed limit is:**

    (a) 55 mph. ❏
    (b) 60 mph. ❏
    (c) 65 mph. ❏
    (d) 70 mph. ❏

10. **A sign on the back of a lorry with red and yellow diagonal stripes and the words 'Long Vehicle' means that the vehicle is at least:**

    (a) 9 metres long. ❏
    (b) 11 metres long. ❏
    (c) 15 metres long. ❏
    (d) 17 metres long. ❏

11. **You are following a lorry which has a triangular sign hanging on it. The sign has diagonal red and white stripes. This indicates:**

    (a) An overhanging load of more than 2 metres. ❏
    (b) An exceptionally heavy load. ❏
    (c) A wide load. ❏
    (d) A slow moving vehicle. ❏

12. **The picture below shows a road of normal width with some roadworks on the opposite side. There are no traffic lights or any other form of control. You are travelling downhill and your side of the road is clear. Approaching the roadworks is a fully laden goods vehicle. Would you:**

    (a) Continue through at the same speed as it is your right of way. ❏
    (b) Flash your lights and wait to see what the oncoming driver is going to do. ❏
    (c) Check your mirror and give way to the oncoming driver. ❏
    (d) Continue at a slower speed in case you have to stop half way through. ❏

13. You are driving a small commercial vehicle with a restricted rear view and no rear, nearside window. When reversing should you:

    (a) Use both exterior mirrors. ❏
    (b) Take all the goods out of the vehicle. ❏
    (c) Never reverse to the left. ❏
    (d) Always reverse out of a side road. ❏

14. You are in the right-hand lane of a dual carriageway and are approaching a roundabout. In the left-hand lane, there is a large goods vehicle carrying a full load. Should you:

    (a) Hang back so that the lorry driver is aware of your presence. ❏
    (b) Stay alongside the lorry. ❏
    (c) Accelerate to try to beat the lorry to the roundabout. ❏
    (d) Flash your headlights to warn the lorry driver. ❏

15. You are travelling at 65 mph in the left-hand lane of a three-lane motorway and a large goods vehicle is trying to overtake you in the centre lane. Should you:

    (a) Accelerate so that the lorry can move in behind you and then slow down to 65 mph again. ❏
    (b) Move out in front of the lorry so that it can get back into the left lane. ❏
    (c) Slow down a little to allow the lorry to get past more quickly. ❏
    (d) Move across to the far right-hand lane to allow the lorry through. ❏

16. Because motorcycles do not take up so much road space they may:
    (Select two answers)

    (a) Drive in between lanes of traffic. ❏
    (b) Use the hard shoulder on motorways. ❏
    (c) Be more difficult to see at junctions. ❏
    (d) Use cycle lanes. ❏

17. You are driving along in traffic and hear the siren of an ambulance. You cannot yet see from which direction the ambulance is approaching. Should you:

    (a) Do nothing until you can see where the ambulance is. ❑

    (b) Check your mirrors, signal if necessary and pull over as ❑ far to the left as you can.

    (c) Accelerate to the next junction and turn off out of danger. ❑

    (d) Flash your lights at the driver in front in case the siren ❑ has not been heard.

18. It is a windy day and you are driving across a viaduct. You decide to overtake the high-sided vehicle ahead of you. Should you: (Select three answers)

    (a) Expect to feel a pull on the steering wheel as you pass it. ❑

    (b) Expect to be buffeted and your car to wander slightly. ❑

    (c) Hold the steering wheel more loosely to compensate. ❑

    (d) Hold the steering wheel more firmly to compensate. ❑

19. Large, heavily-laden goods vehicles sometimes take a long while to drive up steep hills. To compensate for this, some main roads have:

    (a) A total ban on large goods vehicles. ❑

    (b) A total ban on overtaking for large goods vehicles. ❑

    (c) Crawler lanes on the left. ❑

    (d) Crawler lanes on the right. ❑

20. Following a very large vehicle you: (Select two answers)

    (a) Are protected from side winds. ❑

    (b) Have a restricted view of the road ahead. ❑

    (c) Can use them for protection when moving into ❑ roundabouts.

    (d) Should keep well back. ❑

21. In very windy conditions cyclists and motorcyclists may get blown sideways. To compensate for this, should you:

    (a) Allow extra room when overtaking. ❑

    (b) Sound your horn to warn them of your presence. ❑

    (c) Never overtake them in these conditions. ❑

    (d) Drive as closely as you can to protect them from the wind. ❑

22. A fully-laden goods vehicle will:
(Select two answers)

(a) Be able to stop in a shorter distance than when it is ❏
empty.
(b) Take longer to stop on the level than when it is empty. ❏
(c) Slow down considerably when travelling uphill. ❏
(d) Take longer to move off when travelling downhill. ❏

23. On three-lane motorways large goods vehicles are allowed to:

(a) Use all three lanes, if the right-hand lane is used only ❏
for overtaking purposes.
(b) Use the left and centre lanes only. ❏
(c) Drive up to a speed limit of 70 mph. ❏
(d) Drive more closely to the vehicle in front. ❏

24. **If you are towing a caravan, the maximum number of people allowed to travel in the caravan is:**

   (a) None. ❏
   (b) Two. ❏
   (c) As many as would normally travel in the car. ❏
   (d) One adult with two children. ❏

25. **You are towing a caravan and are about to overtake a high-sided lorry. You should allow for:**

   (a) Your car to slow down because of the other vehicle. ❏
   (b) The effect of buffeting and turbulence. ❏
   (c) The other vehicle to move out of your way. ❏
   (d) The other vehicle to slow down for you. ❏

26. **When towing a caravan or wide trailer, what extra precautions can be taken to obtain better all-round vision?**

   (a) Move your head about more as you are driving. ❏
   (b) Get your front seat passenger to help with observations. ❏
   (c) Always drive in the left hand lane on motorways. ❏
   (d) Fit extender arms to the door mirrors. ❏

27. **You have borrowed a van which has an overall height of ten feet. When parking it, you should:**

   (a) Leave it outside the owner's home. ❏
   (b) Leave it in a bus lay-by if there is one nearby. ❏
   (c) Be aware that, if there is a steep camber, the van may tilt and overhang the pavement. ❏
   (d) Park well away from kerb so as not to overhang. ❏

28. **To get the best view before deciding to overtake a large vehicle, you should:**

   (a) Move out to the right as far as possible. ❏
   (b) Keep a good distance back from the vehicle. ❏
   (c) Move as close as possible to shorten overtaking time. ❏
   (d) Speed up so that following drivers don't overtake you. ❏

29. **You are travelling along a main road and you see a bus starting to emerge from a road on the right. You should:**

   (a) Accelerate quickly by to get out of the possible danger. ❏
   (b) Check the mirrors, move over to the left and slow down to allow for the bus pulling out. ❏
   (c) Keep going at the same speed, but flash your headlights to warn the bus driver of your presence. ❏
   (d) Move further over to the right, to prevent the bus . driver from emerging. ❏

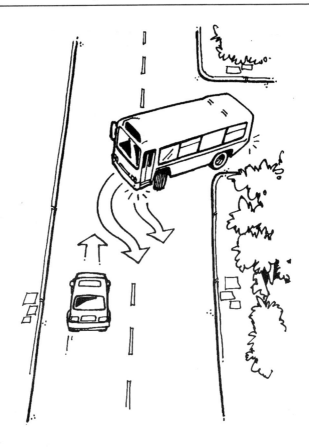

30. Driving along a motorway in heavy rain, expect large vehicles to:

(a) Stay in the left hand lane. ☐
(b) Slow down to 50 mph. ☐
(c) Throw up lots of spray. ☐
(d) Use high intensity rear lights. ☐

⟨∘ANSWERS∘⟩

1. The correct answer is (c).

Every rule in *The Highway Code* is designed so that your driving does not cause any inconvenience or danger to yourself, your passengers or any other road user. If you are driving a large or slow-moving vehicle, whether for pleasure or business, you must accept that the journey is going to take longer than if you were driving a car.

You should always give consideration to other road users. How would you feel if someone was holding you up unnecessarily? If you cause inconvenience, then the other driver may, out of sheer frustration, decide to overtake you where it is not safe. This, in turn, could put you, your passengers, other road users, as well as the overtaking driver, all at risk.

Refer to: *The Highway Code*, rule 53.

2. The correct answers are (a), (c) and (d).

Bus drivers, like any other drivers, sometimes make mistakes. Do not always expect to see signals when they should be used. Because you should be looking for passengers walking out in front of the bus, you should not drive past quickly. If the bus looks as if it is going to move away, check your mirrors, and if it is convenient, give way – after all, it's bigger than you are!

Refers: *The Highway Code*, rule 79; *Learn to Drive in 10 Easy Stages*, Stage 8, page 137.

3. The correct answer is (a).

You should always stay far enough behind a large vehicle so that you can see the road ahead. This is even more important on newly surfaced roads where there is a danger of loose chippings being thrown up by the vehicle ahead. Having your windscreen shattered is inconvenient, to say the least. Flashing your lights will not serve any purpose in this situation. If you are following a car onto this type of surface, you should still keep well back, especially if it is travelling faster than the sign advises. Keep your speed down too, so that you don't throw up any chippings. You should not really be thinking about overtaking on this kind of surface.

Refer to: *The Driving Manual*, Section 8, page 168.

4. The correct answer is (b).

Large vehicles need more room to manoeuvre, especially when turning into narrow side roads. Expect them to swing wide in the opposite direction of the signal to allow for this.

Refer to: *The Highway Code*, rule 107; *The Driving Manual*, Section 8, page 168.

5. The correct answer is (d).

You must wait to see what the lorry driver is going to do. It could be dangerous to pull out if you can't see – the lorry may be obscuring other traffic in the main road. It may not be possible for the lorry to complete its turn while you are still there. You will therefore need to be ready to move if necessary.

Refer to: *Learn to Drive in 10 Easy Stages*, Stage 8, page 136.

6. The correct answer is (c).

The laden weight of a trailer or caravan should never be more than the kerbside weight of the towing vehicle. Ideally, actual weight should not be more than 85% of the empty weight of the towing vehicle.

Refer to: *The Driving Manual*, Section 16, page 280.

7. The correct answer is (d).

The overall weight of the car and trailer combination has been increased to nearly twice the original car weight. This means that the engine will need a considerable amount of power to overtake another vehicle and this is generally regarded as three times the normal time and distance.

Refer to: *The Driving Manual*, Section 16, page 280.

8. The correct answer is (a).

The stability of the outfit is dependent on correct distribution of the weight. By placing heavier items roughly over the axle, you can make sure that the 'nose weight' will be suitable.

Refer to: *The Driving Manual*, Section 16, page 281.

9. The correct answer is (b).

When you tow a trailer you are not allowed to use the right-hand lane of a three-lane motorway and the speed limit is 60 mph.
Refer to: *The Highway Code*, 'Speed Limit' table.

10. The correct answer is (b).

Any goods vehicle longer than 13 metres *must* carry this sign and a goods vehicle over 11 metres *may* carry it.
Refer to: *The Highway Code*, section entitled 'Vehicle Markings'.

11. The correct answer is (a).

Projection markers are triangular with red and white diagonal stripes. They are hung at the rear and on the sides of any loads which overhang the front or rear of a vehicle by more than 2 metres.
Refer to: *The Highway Code*, section entitled 'Vehicle Markings'.

12. The correct answer is (c).

You should have learnt by some of the questions in other sections that safe driving means never assuming another driver will do the correct thing and give way to you – even if it is your priority! Remember, flashing your lights should only be used to warn others of your presence – not as a 'come on!' nor a 'wait there!'. Your message may be misunderstood.
It can be very difficult to get a large vehicle moving uphill, especially if it is fully laden. It would therefore be courteous for you to check your mirrors and wait for the lorry to clear the roadworks.
Refer to: *The Driving Manual*, Section 5, page 88.

13. The correct answer is (a).

When you are driving a vehicle with no effective view to the rear, you should use both mirrors to give as much vision as possible. If necessary get someone to assist.
Refer to *Your Driving Test*, 'The Officially Recommended Syllabus for Learning to Drive'.

14. The correct answer is (a).

You should try to keep back in a position where the lorry driver can see you. To accelerate may put you in danger, especially if you can't proceed because of traffic. If you stay alongside the lorry you could well be in the driver's blind area and he may take an unusual course in the roundabout being totally unaware of your presence. Flashing your headlights will serve absolutely no purpose – particularly if the lorry driver is not using the mirrors.

Refer to: *The Driving Manual*, Section 8, page 168.

15. The correct answer is (c).

You should not feel inadequate simply because a lorry driver wants to pass you. The only safe and sensible option is to let it pass as quickly as possible by slowing down a little. The lorry is obviously travelling faster than you are. If you accelerate to allow for it to move in behind you, but you then slow down, you will be in the same situation. You should not move out across two lanes to let the lorry through – you cannot see what may be in the right-hand lane.

Refer to: *The Driving Manual*, Section 9, page 188.

16. The correct answers are (a) and (c).

In slow-moving traffic or congested areas, motorcyclists and cyclists can often be riding in between lanes. Because they are not very big, they can be difficult to see at junctions. Keep in touch with what is happening all around by using all of your mirrors. Pay particular attention to your observations. Be positive it is clear before moving out: 'Think Once, Think Twice, Think Bike.'

Cycle tracks were designed for cycles not motorbikes! The hard shoulder should only be used in emergencies. But always expect the unexpected.

Refer to: *The Driving Manual*, Section 8, page 173; *The Highway Code*, rule 123.

17. The correct answer is (b).

If you cannot yet see the ambulance you don't know where it is! Take care – it could come up quickly from behind. You should not be accelerating to the next junction, this will not help the ambulance driver if you can't get there before it catches up. Flashing your lights at the driver ahead could be misread. Check that it is safe and pull over to the left – someone's life may be at stake!

Refer to: *The Driving Manual*, Section 12, page 238; *The Highway Code*, rule 76.

18. The correct answers are (a), (b) and (d).

In these conditions you will feel the effect of the wind through the steering and the car being buffeted. If you loosen your grip on the wheel the effect will be worsened and you could be blown into the path of another vehicle. You will need to hold it more firmly to compensate.

Refer to: *The Driving Manual*, Section 10, page 209; *Learn to Drive in 10 Easy Stages*, Stage 8, page 152.

19. The correct answer is (c).

There is no ban on goods vehicles on main roads unless diversions are in operation. If there was a total ban on large vehicles overtaking, this would mean that those which could travel faster than the slowly moving ones would be prevented from making progress. Crawler lanes are sometimes provided on the left to allow faster traffic to pass in relative safety on the right.

Refer to: *The Highway Code*, rule 88.

20. The correct answers are (b) and (d).

Following a very large vehicle will not protect you from side winds. Your view of the road ahead will be restricted, you should therefore keep well back to get a better view. It is dangerous to use any other vehicle as protection when moving into roundabouts. You should only make a decision to proceed when you are absolutely sure that it is safe.

Refer to: *The Driving Manual*, Section 8, page 168; *Learn to Drive in 10 Easy Stages*, Stage 7, page 88.

21. The correct answer is (a).

If you sound your horn in windy conditions it is unlikely to be heard by cyclists, or by motorcyclists because of their helmets. You should not drive too closely to them because this is likely to make them wobble even more. Wait until it is absolutely safe and then overtake if necessary, allowing extra room.

Refer to: *The Highway Code*, rule 101; *The Driving Manual*, Section 8, page 173.

22. The correct answers are (b) and (c).

Because the required distance to stop depends on the size and weight of your vehicle, the heavier the vehicle the longer it will take to stop. Because of the principle of gravity, lorries slow down considerably when going uphill but will speed up much more quickly when travelling downhill. Remember to make allowances for this and drive defensively.

Refer to: *The Driving Manual*, Section 5, page 85.

23. The correct answer is (b).

Large goods vehicles may only use the left hand and centre lanes of a three-lane motorway. They must not use the right-hand lane at all, not even if the left and centre lanes are congested with vehicles moving more slowly. The speed limit for large goods vehicles on motorways is 60 mph. If they drive more closely to the vehicle in front they will not have sufficient stopping distance, particularly if they are fully laden.

Refer to: *The Highway Code*, pages 53 and 71.

24. The correct answer is (a).

You should not allow any passengers to travel in a towed caravan as this would be unsafe. They could be thrown around in the van and sustain injuries.

Refer to: *The Driving Manual*, Section 16, page 283.

25. The correct answer is (b).

When you are towing a caravan you need to take extra care when overtaking, or when you are being overtaken by, a high-sided vehicle. Extra space will be needed to allow for your trailer being blown off its straight course by the air turbulence.

Refer to: *The Driving Manual*, Section 16, page 283.

26. The correct answer is (d).

Normal car door mirrors will not give you a wide enough zone of vision to the rear. You should fit exterior towing mirrors.

Refer to: *The Driving Manual*, Section 16, page 280.

27. The correct answer is (c).

It may not always be convenient to park the vehicle near the owner's home. You should certainly not park in a bus stop – these are intended for buses! If you park well away from the kerb, you will be causing an obstruction in the road. You should be aware that a large vehicle will overhang the pavement if there is a steep camber – this will cause inconvenience to pedestrians.

Refer to: *The Highway Code*, rule 140.

28. The correct answer is (b).

Moving out to the right as far as possible before you know it is safe will put you and any oncoming driver in danger. Moving in as close as possible will only restrict your view of the road ahead. Speeding up before you have decided that it is safe to overtake will only result in you getting too close to the vehicle. Keeping a good distance back will open up your view of the road ahead.

Refer to: *The Driving Manual*, Section 5, page 90.

29. The correct answer is (b).

You should never assume other drivers will do the correct thing. You should remember that a larger vehicle will need more room when turning in and out of junctions – they will also need a little more time than a car. This means that at busy times of the day it may be extremely difficult for them to wait for a large enough gap in the traffic. Flashing your lights may be misinterpreted and going at the same speed could put you in danger – as will moving further out to the right. The courteous action would be to move into the left, slow down and allow the bus driver to pull out.

Refer to: *Learn to Drive in 10 Easy Stages*, Stage 8, page 136.

30. The correct answer is (c).

You can't always expect other drivers to follow the rules regarding lights. Neither should you expect drivers of large vehicles to stay in the left lane nor to drive at 50 mph. They will certainly throw up large amounts of spray, which can greatly reduce your visibility. Keep well back!

Refer to: *The Driving Manual*, Section 10, page 207.

SECTION·8

To become a safe and responsible driver, you do not have to be a mechanical 'whiz kid'! However, it will be your responsibility to make sure the car you are driving is in a legal and roadworthy condition, irrespective of whether you are the owner.

It is important that you:

- know about the driver's legal responsibilites;
- know a little about how the car works;
- are able to make essential everyday checks;
- are able to detect some common faults.

All of these things will ensure that you do not drive a vehicle in an illegal condition or one which may result in a breakdown or damage.

The Highway Code states that there are regulations requiring different parts of your vehicle to be kept in good condition and working order. These include:

- brakes;
- steering;
- lights and indicators;
- windscreens, windows, washers and wipers;
- exhaust systems;
- seatbelts and fittings;
- speedometer and horn;
- tyres;
- bodywork.

Your driving instructor should show you how to check all of the above and to carry out simple jobs such as replacing a bulb or adjusting the tyre pressures. You never know when you are going to get a puncture, so knowing how to change a wheel can save you a lot of time and money.

Before answering the questions in this section read:

- *The Highway Code* – rule: 133, pages: 68 and 91, points 65 and 66.
- *The Driving Manual* – pages: 204, 215, 245, 250, 252, 253, 254, 256, 266 and 317.
- *Learn to Drive in 10 Easy Stages* – pages: 162–4.

You can find out more information about the vehicle you are driving by reading the manufacturer's handbook. If you are really keen, you might think about attending a basic car maintenance course at your local college of further education.

∘QUESTIONS∘

Remember only to select one answer unless indicated otherwise.

1. **When deciding on the type of oil to put in your car engine, should you:**

   (a) Always choose a multigrade oil. ❏
   (b) Use two-stroke oil. ❏
   (c) Make sure you use the oil recommended in the vehicle handbook. ❏
   (d) Look around for what's on special offer at the local garages. ❏

2. **The lubricating oil in the gearbox of a modern vehicle should:**

   (a) Be drained off and changed at every service interval. ❏
   (b) Never need changing. ❏
   (c) Be exactly the same as that used in the engine. ❏
   (d) Be checked at service intervals. ❏

3. **When driving in wintry conditions, if your windscreen freezes over while the car is parked you should:**

   (a) Pour boiling water over it to melt the ice. ❏
   (b) Clean it off with antifreeze. ❏
   (c) Use your cigarette lighter turned up fully as a blowtorch. ❏
   (d) Use a scraper or a special de-icer spray to clear the ice off. ❏

4. **If your radiator starts to overheat while you are driving, should you:**

    (a) Pour cold water over it as soon as possible. ❑
    (b) Drive to the nearest garage to get it looked at. ❑
    (c) Never remove the cap while it is still hot. ❑
    (d) Drive more slowly to give it a chance to cool down. ❑

5. **The amount of antifreeze you will need to use will be:**

    (a) Four pints for a car with a large engine. ❑
    (b) One litre every month. ❑
    (c) Shown in the vehicle handbook. ❑
    (d) Dependent on how much driving you do. ❑

6. **If you find that the handbrake will not hold the car stationary on steep hills, you are advised to:**

    (a) Get the handbrake adjusted. ❑
    (b) Use the footbrake to hold you stationary. ❑
    (c) Leave the car in gear and you won't need the handbrake. ❑
    (d) Use a route that bypasses all the steep hills. ❑

7. **If you are in any doubt about the efficiency of your vehicle's braking system, should you:**

    (a) Test it by simulating an emergency stop at high speed. ❑
    (b) Call out the local breakdown service. ❑
    (c) Not use the car and have it checked immediately. ❑
    (d) Continue driving but use your brakes gently and progressively. ❑

8. **You should check the condition of your tyres each time you're going to drive. The pressures should be checked at least:**

    (a) Every time you are going to drive it. ❑
    (b) After a long journey. ❑
    (c) Each week. ❑
    (d) When the car is serviced. ❑

9. **The minimum legal tread depth on a car tyre is:**

    (a) 1 millimetre. ❏
    (b) 1.6 millimetres. ❏
    (c) 2 millimetres. ❏
    (d) 2.6 millimetres. ❏

10. **If you feel the car pulling over to one side with a bumping sensation should you:**

    (a) Stop gradually at the roadside and check for a flat tyre. ❏
    (b) Steer off the road and onto the pavement out of danger. ❏
    (c) Drive to the nearest garage. ❏
    (d) Brake as hard as you can and stop where you are. ❏

11. **You should make regular checks of:**

    (a) The amount of oil in the gearbox. ❏
    (b) The amount of antifreeze in the cooling system. ❏
    (c) The water level in the cooling system. ❏
    (d) The brake fluid reservoir. ❏

12. **After changing a wheel, you notice a vibration in the steering. This is likely to be caused by:**

   (a) Driving over a bumpy road surface. ❏
   (b) The new tyre having more tread. ❏
   (c) There being a fault in the steering system. ❏
   (d) The wheelnuts have not been properly tightened. ❏

13. **Knowing a little about how your car works and how to detect some of the minor defects will:**

   (a) Help you drive it more economically and sympathetically. ❏
   (b) Ensure that you pass the Driving Test first time. ❏
   (c) Ensure that you are never involved in an accident. ❏
   (d) Mean that you never have to take it to a garage for repairs. ❏

14. **If you are driving a car with a diesel engine the correct fuel to use is:**

   (a) Unleaded petrol. ❏
   (b) Diesel only. ❏
   (c) Liquid petroleum gas. ❏
   (d) Two-stroke petrol. ❏

15. **Different fuels burn at different temperatures. If you use the wrong type of fuel you could:**

   (a) Save money by choosing the cheapest. ❏
   (b) Get more mileage per gallon. ❏
   (c) Be prosecuted. ❏
   (d) Damage the valves and cylinder head. ❏

16. **Filters and spark plugs should be changed:**

   (a) At least once a month. ❏
   (b) At the recommended intervals. ❏
   (c) Only if you drive more than 1,000 miles per month. ❏
   (d) Whenever you top up the oil in the engine. ❏

17. Tyres should be:

    (a) Free of cuts, bulges and other defects. ❑

    (b) Changed round every week. ❑

    (c) Fitted with radials on the nearside and crossply on the ❑
        offside.

    (d) Over-inflated in bad weather. ❑

18. Your car fails the MOT test and you want to continue to use it. You need to:

    (a) Apply to the DVLA for a certificate. ❑

    (b) Wait one month for a re-test. ❑

    (c) Wait until the tax is renewed. ❑

    (d) Make prior arrangements for a re-test. ❑

19. Which of the following would cause failure on the MOT test:

    (a) Lack of water in the screen wash container. ❑

    (b) A slight slackness in the steering. ❑

    (c) A torn seat. ❑

    (d) A tyre with 2 mm of tread. ❑

20. If the needle on the temperature gauge on the instrument panel points to hot this means:

    (a) The temperature inside the car is getting too hot. ❑

    (b) The air conditioning system is not working. ❑

    (c) The water in the radiator is not being cooled by the fan. ❑

    (d) The outside temperature is rising. ❑

21. A loose fan belt can cause:

(a) Higher fuel consumption. ❏
(b) An engine to overheat. ❏
(c) Lower fuel consumption. ❏
(d) The brakes to fail. ❏

22. If you get a puncture should you:

(a) Drive to the nearest garage to get it repaired. ❏
(b) Drive home and get the wheel changed as soon as you can. ❏
(c) Stop as soon as possible and get the wheel changed. ❏
(d) Call out the local police to help you. ❏

23. To check the oil level in the engine you need to:

(a) Look at the oil pressure warning light. ❏
(b) Open the bonnet and use the dipstick. ❏
(c) Call out the local breakdown service. ❏
(d) Wait until the car goes in for a service. ❏

24. If you drive a car with an automatic gearbox should you:

(a) Never need to use the handbrake. ❏
(b) Use the handbrake every time you stop. ❏
(c) Be aware that your car may have a tendency to creep. ❏
(d) Only use the handbrake at red traffic lights. ❏

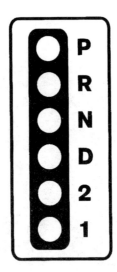

25. Before setting off on a long journey you should check:

(a) Petrol, oil, water, lights and tyres. ❏
(b) Heaters, petrol, oil, water and lights. ❏
(c) Radiator, oil, petrol, brake fluid and seatbelts. ❏
(d) Tyres, footbrake, petrol, handbrake and lights. ❏

26. Which of the following is potentially the most serious:

(a) Low antifreeze level. ❏
(b) Low fuel level. ❏
(c) Low brake fluid level. ❏
(d) Low engine temperature. ❏

27. Antifreeze should be:

(a) Checked at least every 12 months. ❏
(b) Changed every 6 months. ❏
(c) Drained off during summer months. ❏
(d) At double strength during winter months. ❏

28. To top up the battery, you should use:

(a) Boiled tap water. ❏
(b) Distilled water. ❏
(c) Bottled water. ❏
(d) Cold tap water. ❏

29. This warning light on the instrument panel tells you that the:

(a) Headlights are on full beam. ❏
(b) High intensity rear lights are on. ❏
(c) Front fog lights are on. ❏
(d) A bulb has fused. ❏

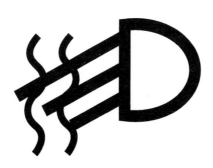

30. **If a brake warning light stays on when you start driving, you should:**

   (a) Only drive as far as the garage to have it checked. ❏
   (b) Not drive until you have checked for the cause. ❏
   (c) Drive only if you use arm signals for slowing down. ❏
   (d) Get the problem fixed within 24 hours. ❏

◦ANSWERS ◦

1. **The correct answer is (c).**

If you use the wrong oil for your car's engine, you could shorten its useful life. Using the cheapest is not always a good investment. As new or reconditioned engines are expensive to buy it makes good financial sense to use the correct oil. Oil is the 'lifeblood' of the car's engine. Would you want the wrong blood-group type coursing through your veins?
Refer to: *The Driving Manual*, Section 13, page 252.

2. **The correct answer is (d).**

Although the amount of oil used in a modern gearbox is minimal, it performs a valuable function and should be checked when the vehicle is serviced – at regular intervals. Always use the oil which is recommended in the vehicle handbook.

3. **The correct answer is (d).**

This is the most effective and safest way of clearing ice from the windscreen. Scrapers and spray de-icer can be purchased from most good vehicle accessory shops. Boiling water could crack the screen; a harsh flame could do the same. Antifreeze would leave smears on the windscreen and be very difficult to clean off – it could even rot the rubber seal around the window.
Refer to: *The Driving Manual*, Section 10, page 215.

4. **The correct answer is (c).**

You should never remove the radiator cap while it is still hot as you could easily get scalded. Wait until it has cooled down before you start investigating the cause of the problem.
As water is used to keep most engines cool, it is important that you check the water level frequently, particularly before setting out on a long journey. Antifreeze can nowadays be left in the radiator all year round. This will help prolong the life of your cooling system.
Refer to: *The Driving Manual*, Section 10, page 253.

5. **The correct answer is (c).**

All vehicles vary. You should check the vehicle handbook to find out how much antifreeze your particular car needs. Some modern cars have sealed radiators but the coolant may be kept in a separate reservoir. The water/antifreeze content of the radiator should be checked every year before winter sets in.
Refer to: *The Driving Manual*, Section 13, page 253.

6. **The correct answer is (a).**

The car is unsafe if the handbrake is not working properly. Get it adjusted. To save wear on the handbrake, do not use excessive force when applying it as this could stretch the cable. For the same reason you should always make sure that you do not apply the handbrake until the car has stopped. When you use the handbrake, make sure you press the ratchet button in so as not to cause this to wear out.
Refer to: *The Driving Manual*, Section 13, page 254; your car's handbook.

7. **The correct answer is (c).**

An efficient braking system is vital to driving safety – do not drive a car if the brakes are not working properly. Regular servicing will help ensure that your brakes are working properly and are safe. Test your brakes every day, but choose a safe place so that you will not inconvenience any other road user.
Refer to: Your vehicle Handbook for frequency of servicing.

8. **The correct answer is (c).**

You should check the condition of your tyres every time you are going to drive your car. After a long journey the tyres will be hot and you will not get a true pressure reading. If you only check them once a month, or only when the car is serviced, they could well have deteriorated in between the checks. Make sure you check the tyre pressure at least once a week, for example when you refuel.
Refer to: *The Driving Manual*, Section 10, page 204; Section 13, page 256. Also check the handbook for the recommended tyre pressures for your car.

9. **The correct answer is (b).**

The legal minimum tread depth for a car tyre is 1.6 mm.
Refer to: *The Highway Code*, page 68.

10. **The correct answer is (a).**

Steering to the side of the road and stopping gradually is the only safe option. Driving to the nearest garage will cause more damage to the tyre and braking hard with a flat tyre would be dangerous. You should certainly not steer onto the pavement as this will damage the tyre more and you could also be endangering pedestrians.
Refer to: *The Driving Manual*, Section 14, page 266.

11. **The correct answer is (c).**

Checking the amount of water in the radiator or cooling system is important. If the level is low the engine could overheat and become damaged. The other items listed can be checked a little less frequently at service intervals as in modern vehicles these items are designed to be more maintenance-free.
Refer to: Your vehicle Handbook.

12. **The correct answer is (d).**

If the problem arose immediately after changing a wheel, the most likely cause is that the wheelnuts were not tightened enough. When you change a wheel always ensure that the nuts are retightened before driving away. If the wheel you have just put on has not been balanced, this could cause vibration at certain speeds.

13. **The correct answer is (a).**

Knowing how the car works will certainly help you develop a sense of vehicle sympathy and economical driving style. It cannot guarantee that you will pass your Driving Test – this will depend on your driving skills. Neither can it guarantee that you will never be involved in an accident or ever have to go to a garage for repairs.

14. The correct answer is (b).

Diesel engines will only run on that type of fuel. Any other type will damage the engine.
Refer to: *The Driving Manual*, Section 13, page 25.

15. The correct answer is (d).

Fuels burn at different temperatures and using the wrong type can damage the valves and cylinder head. You must use the fuel for which the engine was designed. You may think you are saving money by buying the cheapest fuel but it will cost you far more if you have to buy a new engine.

16. The correct answer is (b).

Filters and spark plugs need only be changed at the recommended intervals and this is usually dictated by the mileage. You may not be driving sufficient mileage every month to warrant the replacements. These items should certainly not need changing at 1,000 mile intervals.
Refer to: The handbook of your car for advice.

17. The correct answer is (a).

When tyres are damaged you could get a 'blow-out' at any time. Make sure that they are not damaged in any way by checking them before you drive. It is not necessary to rotate the tyres on a weekly basis. The only legal mix of tyres is crossply on the front axle and radials on the rear axle. The tyre pressures recommended by the manufacturer apply in all weather conditions.

18. The correct answer is (d).

You must not continue to use a car which has failed an MOT test unless you have previously made arrangements for the re-test.
Refer to: *The Driving Manual*, Section 12, page 245.

19. The correct answer is (a).

For information on the MOT test requirements, ask for a list of the items which are tested at your nearest authorised testing station.

20. The correct answer is (c).

This warning light is to inform the driver that the engine cooling system is not working and the radiator is not being cooled down. The most likely cause of this is a worn or broken fan belt, or a loss of water caused by a leak in the system. You should stop as soon as it is safe, as an overheating engine could cause serious damage.

21. The correct answer is (b).

A loose fan belt will have no effect on fuel consumption. Neither will it have any effect on the braking system. It is part of the cooling system and will result in damage through overheating if loose or worn.

22. The correct answer is (c).

If you continue driving on a punctured tyre you will cause more damage, not only to the tyre, but to the wheel rim as well. Stop gradually as soon as you can, driving as slowly as possible to avoid further damage. The local police do not run car recovery services. You can save yourself quite a lot of time and money by learning how to change a wheel for yourself – it is not as difficult as you may think!

Refer to: *The Driving Manual*, Section 14, page 266; *Learn to Drive in 10 Easy Stages*, Stage 9, page 163.

23. The correct answer is (b).

Checking the oil pressure warning light will not tell you how much oil there is in the engine. Although the oil level might be low this light is mainly a warning of the pressure forcing it around the engine. Check your vehicle's handbook for the location of the dipstick under the bonnet. Calling out the local breakdown service would be totally unrealistic – and very expensive – to carry out this simple job. If you wait until the car goes in for its next service and the oil level is low you will be damaging your engine.

Refer to: The handbook of your car; *The Driving Manual*, Section 13, page 252.

24. The correct answer is (c).

Whatever type of car you are driving, it is not essential to use the handbrake for short pauses. However, if you have to wait for more than a few moments in any traffic situation (not just at red traffic lights), you should use it to secure the car. Automatic cars have a tendency to creep. This means you will need to use the handbrake more often than you would in a car with a manual gearbox.

Refer to: *The Driving Manual*, Section 20, page 317; *Learn to Drive in 10 Easy Stages*, Stage 2, page 29.

25. The correct answer is (a).

These items should be checked before you set out on a long journey: make sure you have enough fuel; check the oil level (look for telltale stains under the car); check the water in the washer bottle and the radiator coolant (remember it is far safer to do this now rather than when the water is hot); check that all the lights and indicators are working; and check that the tyres are in good condition and properly inflated.

Refer to: *The Driving Manual*, Section 13, page 252; *Learn to Drive in 10 Easy Stages*, Stage 9, page 163.

26. The correct answer is (c).

Brakes are too important to be ignored – check the fluid regularly. If there is not enough fluid in the reservoir, the brakes may fail. Test your brakes every day. If you hear any strange noises, or if your vehicle pulls to one side, consult a mechanic immediately.

Refer to: *The Driving Manual*, Section 13, page 254.

27. The correct answer is (a).

In modern cars a mixture of water and antifreeze is kept in the radiator all year round. It only needs to be checked every twelve months – the most sensible time would be just before the onset of winter.

Refer to: *The Driving Manual*, Section 13, page 253.

28. The correct answer is (b).

Most modern batteries are maintenance free and sealed for life. If a battery is fitted with a filler cap, check the level and fill up if necessary. Only use distilled water.

Refer to: *The Driving Manual*, Section 13, page 256.

29. The correct answer is (c).

It is important to know what the different warning lights mean. Remember, you should only use fog and high intensity rear lights when visibility falls below 100 metres.

Refer to: *The Highway Code*, rule 133, page 91, point 65; *The Driving Manual*, Section 2, page 35; your vehicle's handbook.

30. The correct answer is (b).

You should not drive if a brake warning light stays on – a dangerous fault may have developed. You should not drive again before having the car checked.

Refer to: *The Highway Code*, page 91, point 66.

SECTION·9

VEHICLE SECURITY AND ENVIRONMENTAL ISSUES

Preservation of our environment is becoming more and more important as exhaust emissions and noise pollution increase with the volume of traffic. There are legal limits relating to all vehicle emissions and it is important that you know about these.

You are responsible for the roadworthiness of the car you are driving, in relation to its effect on the environment. This responsibility applies even if it is not your car.

Conserving energy in all fields of life is becoming increasingly necessary as demands on world resources increase. As a motorist, you need to be aware of the most economic use of your vehicle. Fuel consumption varies, not only according to the size and capacity of your car, but also in relation to the way in which you drive it.

To encourage motorists to use public transport, light rapid transport systems are being introduced into some of the larger cities. You should bear in mind that you may, at some time in your driving career, visit some of these towns. You should therefore know how to apply the rules which relate to these trams.

Because of the speed and volume of today's traffic, methods of slowing drivers down in built-up areas are being introduced into more and more towns. You should be able to recognise the signs and know how to approach these different situations.

You should be aware of the need to be considerate when using the equipment your car has and how it affects other people. For example, there are certain times when using the horn would be most inconsiderate. Having your radio on full volume will not only affect your concentration, but it may also cause problems for others around you.

You should be aware of the need to protect your car from theft as the level of car crime increases. Equipment to help avoid car crime includes:

- burglar alarms;
- steering locks;
- immobilisers – these cut off the fuel supply.

The questions in this section test your knowledge of the ways in which you can protect your car and its contents from crime, and also how the way in which you drive can affect the environment. Before you start answering the questions you should read:

- *The Driving Manual* – pages 39, 70, 71, 103, 165, 175, 231, 241, 242, 246, 250, 251, 252, 276 and 285–7.
- *The Highway Code* – rule 136.
- *Know Your Traffic Signs*, pages 22, 29, 97 and 99.
- *Learn to Drive in 10 Easy Stages* – Stage 9.

⦗°QUESTIONS°⦘

Remember to select only one answer unless indicated otherwise.

1. It is a legal requirement that drivers ensure that their exhaust system is efficient. An efficient system is one that:

   (a) Has no holes causing it to 'blow' noisily. ❑
   (b) Has connections which are secure and airtight. ❑
   (c) Has all of the fumes and noise channelled through the ❑
       silencer boxes, which must not be unsuitable or defective.
   (d) Complies with all of the above. ❑

2. If you are driving a vehicle which has a 'worn' engine it is likely to burn a certain amount of oil. You must ensure that it does:

   (a) Not emit excessive amounts of smoke and fumes. ❑
   (b) Not burn more than one pint of oil per week. ❑
   (c) Not burn more than one litre of oil per week. ❑
   (d) Not burn more than two litres of oil per week. ❑

3. Between which of the following times would it be an offence to sound your horn in a built-up area?

   (a) 11.30 pm and 7.00 am. ❑
   (b) 11.00 pm and 8.00 am. ❑
   (c) 7.30 am and 11.30 pm. ❑
   (d) None of these apply if you are letting someone know ❑
       you are waiting for them.

4. Apart from certain times, when is it an offence to sound the horn?

   (a) Outside a police station. ❑
   (b) When turning at junctions where there are pedestrians. ❑
   (c) When driving within the zigzag lines at crossings. ❑
   (d) When stationary, except when in possible danger from ❑
       another moving vehicle.

5. When warning others of your presence, using the horn or flashing your lights:

   (a) Automatically gives you the right of way. ❑
   (b) Does not relieve you of the responsibility to drive safely. ❑
   (c) Is to be avoided in built-up areas. ❑
   (d) Will help to relieve your frustration when driving. ❑

6. **If you have to park your car unattended at night, you should try to leave it:**

   (a) In a well lit area. ❏

   (b) In the corner of a dark car park so it is out of sight. ❏

   (c) On the wrong side of the road to be seen better by oncoming drivers. ❏

   (d) With your headlights on. ❏

7. **Window etching:**

   (a) Is a security measure. ❏

   (b) Gives a clearer view. ❏

   (c) Is a toughening process for your windows. ❏

   (d) Decorates the glass. ❏

8. **Fuel consumption can be improved, that is, you can get more miles to the gallon, if you:**

   (a) Use unleaded fuel. ❏

   (b) Use your car for short trips only. ❏

   (c) Use all of the controls smoothly. ❏

   (d) Coast when you are driving down hills. ❏

9. **When leaving your vehicle unattended, you should:**

   (a) Leave the doors unlocked so that thieves will not damage the locks. ❏

   (b) Remove all valuables or lock them in the boot out of sight. ❏

   (c) Make sure the children are locked inside but have a window open. ❏

   (d) Leave any valuables on the floor. ❏

10. **A car thief is less likely to break into a car which:**

   (a) Has an alarm or visible security device. ❏

   (b) Is over three years old. ❏

   (c) Does not look very valuable. ❏

   (d) Is not very powerful. ❏

11. If a car is fitted with a catalytic converter, this means that:

(a) The car will use 50% less fuel. ❏
(b) Only unleaded fuel should be used. ❏
(c) The gearbox is semi-automatic. ❏
(d) The steering will be lighter. ❏

12. Diesel engines are:

(a) More environmentally friendly than petrol engines. ❏
(b) Less environmentally friendly than petrol engines. ❏
(c) About the same. ❏
(d) Only used in commercial vehicles. ❏

13. Fuel can be saved by driving at slower speeds. For example, driving at a constant speed of 70 mph uses more fuel than driving at a constant 50 mph. This difference can be as much as:

(a) 20%. ❏
(b) 30%. ❏
(c) 40%. ❏
(d) 50%. ❏

14. There are numerous anti-theft devices available, many of which are now fitted as standard equipment. Immobilisers are fitted to:

(a) Prevent the engine from being started by cutting off the fuel supply. ❏
(b) Render a thief immobile when trying to steal your car. ❏
(c) Lock up the rear wheels so the car cannot be moved. ❏
(d) Make sure the car cannot be moved after the engine has been started by a thief. ❏

15. 'Supertrams' or 'Light Rapid Transport Systems' are being introduced in some larger towns and cities to encourage more drivers to leave their cars at home. The signs indicating speed limits to tram drivers are:

(a) Circular in shape. ❏
(b) Diamond shaped. ❏
(c) Rectangular. ❏
(d) Triangular. ❏

16. Traffic calming is an expression used to describe:

(a) A physical means of slowing down traffic. ❏

(b) A system of avoiding 'road rage'. ❏

(c) A temporary speed limit on a motorway. ❏

(d) A special type of one-way street. ❏

17. When your car is being serviced, the best way to deal with the waste engine oil is:

(a) Use some of it again by mixing it with the new oil. ❏

(b) Dispose of it at a proper site. ❏

(c) Make sure that it is tipped onto waste ground. ❏

(d) Tip it down a drain. ❏

18. If you drive into an unfamiliar town which has a 'supertram' system in operation, you should deal with these in the same way as you would railway crossings. You should:

(a) Watch out for pedestrian crossings near tram stops. ❏

(b) Try to get past trams as quickly as you can. ❏

(c) Drive between the platforms if there are no trams about. ❏

(d) Watch for the tracks moving from one side of the road to the other. ❏

19. Radios fitted into new cars are mostly 'security coded'. This means:

(a) It is easier to tune in to the different radio stations. ❏

(b) Traffic hold-ups are broadcast on a more regular basis. ❏

(c) The car is less likely to be stolen. ❏

(d) If removed, the radio cannot be used without knowing the radio code. ❏

20. The MOT test now includes a strict exhaust emission test. This means that:

(a) The engine must be correctly tuned and adjusted. ❏

(b) You should only use unleaded fuel. ❏

(c) Your car engine should not be more than 1800 cc. ❏

(d) You need to service your own car regularly. ❏

21. **Every car has a 'Vehicle Registration Document'. When you buy a used car you must, as soon as possible, for security reasons:**

   (a) Record your details and send the document back to the previous owner. ❑

   (b) Obtain the driving licence details of the previous owner. ❑

   (c) Send the document off to the DVLA, Swansea, with your details. ❑

   (d) Notify the local police that you are now the owner of this car. ❑

22. **If you are travelling alone at night through a busy area and feel uncomfortable about your personal security it is a good idea to:**

   (a) Keep the windows open so that you can attract attention if necessary. ❑

   (b) Lock all the doors. ❑

   (c) Drive with only the sidelights on. ❑

   (d) Keep the radio on full volume. ❑

23. **'Rumble devices' are often used in rural areas. Their purpose is to:**

   (a) Deter potential car thieves. ❑

   (b) Test a car's suspension. ❑

   (c) Alert drivers to a hazard ahead. ❑

   (d) Stop animals from wandering into the road. ❑

24. **You are driving home at midnight from a party in town. You think a driver is about to pull out from a junction into your path, should you:**
(Select two answers)

   (a) Check your mirror, slow down and proceed only when you are sure it is safe. ❑

   (b) Sound your horn to warn the other driver of your presence. ❑

   (c) Flash your headlights to warn of your presence. ❑

   (d) Keep going at the same speed. ❑

25. **To help protect the environment you should:**
(Select two answers)

   (a) Make sure you use as much unleaded fuel as possible. ❑

   (b) Make sure your vehicle is properly tuned and serviced. ❑

   (c) Make sure you use the controls smoothly and avoid harsh braking. ❑

   (d) Use your car for short journeys only. ❑

26. If you don't want your vehicle to be stolen, you should:
(Select three answers)

(a) Fit an alarm to it. ❑

(b) Never leave it unattended. ❑

(c) Make sure it is secure. ❑

(d) Fit an immobiliser. ❑

(e) Never park it in the street. ❑

27. Exhaust systems should:

(a) Eliminate all engine emissions. ❑

(b) Reduce emissions to prescribed levels. ❑

(c) Be fitted with twin baffle pipes. ❑

(d) Be checked at least every week. ❑

28. The amount of oil an engine uses will depend on:
(Select three answers)

(a) The amount of wear and usage. ❑

(b) How you drive the car. ❑

(c) The brand of oil which you use. ❑

(d) Whether your car is petrol or diesel fuelled. ❑

(e) The type of engine. ❑

29. Cars fitted with catalytic converters may use:

(a) Either leaded or unleaded fuel. ❑

(b) Diesel fuel only. ❑

(c) Unleaded petrol only. ❑

(d) Four-star petrol only. ❑

30. You may use the hazard warning lights to warn others, if:
(Select two answers)

(a) Your car has broken down and cannot be moved. ❑

(b) Your car has broken down and is being towed. ❑

(c) You have to slow down quickly on a motorway. ❑

(d) You need to park for a short time on double yellow lines. ❑

⦗○ANSWERS○⦘

1. **The correct answer is (d).**

   Under the Road Vehicles (Construction and Use) Regulations 1986 it is an offence to drive with a defective exhaust system. The system should not pollute the environment either with fumes or excessive noise.
   Refer to: *The Driving Manual*, Section 12, page 241.

2. **The correct answer is (a).**

   Road Vehicles (Construction and Use) Regulations 1986 apply. Oil is the 'lifeblood' of the motor car. It is vital for the smooth running of the car. To ensure that you are not polluting the atmosphere, should you:

   - check the oil regularly;
   - use the correct oil for the vehicle;
   - use the correct amount of oil;
   - change the oil regularly.

   Refer to: *The Driving Manual*, Section 13, pages 251 and 252. Your vehicle's handbook will give you specific information about which oil to use and how much.

3. **The correct answer is (a).**

   Your driving instructor will teach you how, why and when to sound the horn. It should only be used when your vehicle is moving and you need to warn other road users that you are there. The horn should not normally be used when your vehicle is stationary unless you are in possible danger from another moving vehicle. You should not sound your horn when passing hospitals or animals. The horn should never be used in an aggressive manner.
   Refer to: *The Highway Code*, rule 136.

4. **The correct answer is (d).**

The horn can be very useful in situations where other road users, particularly pedestrians, may not have seen you. It is better to sound the horn lightly to prevent someone stepping out in front of your car, than having to carry out an emergency stop. However, sounding the horn unnecessarily could inconvenience someone. For example, using the horn to let someone know you are picking them up, could be very annoying to a night-worker who has just gone to sleep after a hard shift in a factory.

Refer to: *The Highway Code*, rule 136; *The Driving Manual*, Section 5, page 70; Section 8, pages 165 and 175.

5. **The correct answer is (b).**

If you are driving safely, and anticipating correctly, you should seldom need to flash your lights or sound the horn. However, if you think that other road users have not seen you, do not be frightened to use it in a 'defensive' way. However, using the horn does not take away your obligation to avoid accidents whenever possible!

Refer to: *The Driving Manual*, Section 5, pages 70 and 71.

6. **The correct answer is (a).**

You should always try to leave your car parked in a well lit area.
Refer to: *The Driving Manual*, Section 17.

7. **The correct answer is (a).**

Window etching is one of the ways of deterring thieves. The car's registration number is etched into all of the windows so that it can be easily recognised.

Refer to: *The Driving Manual*, Section 17.

8. **The correct answer is (c).**

Using all of the controls smoothly and progressively will give you more miles per gallon. Mileage per gallon is generally reduced on shorter trips as there is generally more stopping and starting, and the engine does not get warmed up properly so is therefore working at less efficiency. Under no circumstances should you coast – your car is not under proper control.

Refer to: *The Driving Manual*, Section 15, page 276.

9. **The correct answer is (b).**

If you have to leave valuables in the car you should put them in the boot where they cannot be seen. Leaving the doors unlocked will encourage theft. Children should not be left in an unattended car. Leaving valuables on the floor where they can be seen will be an open invitation to a thief.

Refer to: *The Driving Manual*, Section 17.

10. **The correct answer is (a).**

A thief is far less likely to attempt to steal a car which has an alarm fitted. Thieves do not discriminate when it comes to taking other people's property – they will take anything that is available.

Refer to: *The Driving Manual*, Section 17.

11. **The correct answer is (b).**

Leaded fuel should never be used in a car which has a catalytic converter. Even a small amount can damage the system.

Refer to: *The Driving Manual*, Section 13, page 250.

12. **The correct answer is (a).**

Diesel engines are generally more environmentally friendly than petrol engines.

Refer to: *The Driving Manual*, Section 15, page 250.

13. **The correct answer is (b).**

More fuel economy is achieved by driving at lower constant speeds.

Refer to: *The Driving Manual*, Section 15, page 276.

14. **The correct answer is (a).**

Immobilisers are fitted to cut off the fuel supply from the engine.
Refer to: The handbook of your vehicle.

15. The correct answer is (b).

If you carried out your studies properly for Section 3 of this book, you should know that circular shaped signs give orders, rectangular signs give information and triangular signs give warnings. This only leaves the diamond-shaped signs which are for tram drivers.

Refer to: *Know Your Traffic Signs*, page 29.

16. The correct answer is (a).

Various devices are used to achieve traffic calming in urban areas where there is likely to be pedestrian activity. These include: road humps, road narrowing, extending kerbs out – combined with special markings, give way priorities, and textured, coloured surfaces. Warning signs are normally erected at the beginning of roads where traffic calming measures are in force.

Refer to: *Know Your Traffic Signs*, page 97.

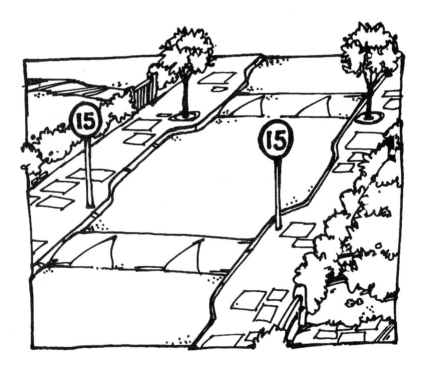

17. The correct answer is (b).

Used engine oil should be disposed of at a recognised site which has facilities. It should not be re-used in the car, and should not be poured away, either down a drain or on waste ground, as this will cause contamination.

18. The correct answers are (a) and (d).

You should certainly not try to get past trams as quickly as possible. There may not be enough room, especially if the tracks change direction and you cannot see them very well. It would be dangerous, even if there were no trams about, to drive between platforms.
Refer to: *The Driving Manual*, Section 5, page 103.

19. The correct answer is (d).

A car radio which is 'security coded' is less likely to be stolen than one which is not. The system is designed so that if the radio is removed and refitted into another vehicle it will not work unless you know what the code is.
Refer to: *The Driving Manual*, Section 17, page 287.

20. The correct answer is (a).

Exhaust emissions are now tested as part of the annual MOT test. Roadside checks are also carried out by the Department of Transport. If your car is correctly tuned and properly adjusted on a regular basis, there should be no problem with either of these tests. Unleaded petrol is more environmentally friendly. However, many cars run on leaded petrol without emitting unnecessarily high readings of exhaust gases.
Refer to: *The Driving Manual*, Section 12, page 246.

21. The correct answer is (c).

It is a legal requirement that Vehicle Registration Documents are sent to DVLA giving details of new ownership. Although this document is not necessarily proof of ownership, it does show who is the 'registered keeper' of the vehicle and is, therefore, a useful security document. It should not be kept with the vehicle.
Refer to: *The Driving Manual*, Section 12, page 242.

22. The correct answer is (b).

It is often sensible, for security reasons, that you keep the doors locked and the windows closed. You should also make sure that any items of value, such as cameras, briefcases, handbags or portable telephones, are kept out of sight.

Refer to: *The Driving Manual*, Section 17, page 287.

23. The correct answer is (c).

Rumble devices, which are often raised strips across the road, are used to encourage drivers to reduce speed because of a hazard ahead. These ridges can be felt and heard to alert drivers to the potential hazard.

Refer to: *Know Your Traffic Signs*, page 99.

24. The correct answers are (a) and (c).

To show consideration to others, noise at night should be kept to an absolute minimum. Because of this it is an offence to use the horn, in any circumstances, between the hours of 11.30 pm and 7.00 am. You could flash the headlights to warn the other driver of your presence. However, this may not necessarily mean the other driver will do the correct thing, so check your mirrors and slow down in case he pulls out.

Refer to: *The Driving Manual*, Section 11, page 231.

25. The correct answers are (b) and (c).

If your car is not designed to use unleaded fuel, using it will damage the engine. Using the car for short journeys uses more fuel – you should use public transport, cycle or walk. Make sure your car is properly tuned, this will result in more economical use of fuel, as will using the controls smoothly.

Refer to: *The Driving Manual*, Section 15, page 276.

26. The correct answers are (a), (c) and (d).

It would be unrealistic never to leave your car unattended and it is sometimes necessary to park in a street. You should have an alarm and/or immobiliser fitted to deter potential thieves. When the car is left unattended make sure that it is securely locked and that any valuable items are stowed out of sight in the boot.

Refer to: *The Driving Manual*, Section 17, page 285.

27. The correct answer is (b).

It would be impossible to eliminate all engine emissions. However, there are now prescribed legal levels and cars are checked for this on the MOT test. It is not really necessaray to check exhaust systems every week, nor to fit all cars with twin baffle pipes.

Refer to: *The Driving Manual*, Section 12, page 246.

28. The correct answers are (a), (b) and (c).

The more mileage your car covers the more oil it will use, as with fuel. The size and type of engine will also affect oil usage. If the car is not tuned properly it will use more oil. If you do not drive smoothly, using all of the controls effectively, you will also have to top up with oil more often.

Refer to: *The Driving Manual*, Section 13, page 251.

29. The correct answer is (c).

You should only use unleaded fuel in vehicles with catalytic converters. Using leaded fuel or diesel will cause damage.

Refer to: *The Driving Manual*, Section 13, page 250.

30. The correct answers are (a) and (c).

Hazard warning lights should not be used on a vehicle being towed. A following driver would not have any warning when it is going to turn right or left. They should not be used as an excuse to park illegally. It cannot be helped if your car has broken down, but you need to warn others that it is causing an obstruction. Similarly if there is a sudden slowing down of fast traffic on a motorway, you need to draw the problem quickly to the attention of following drivers.

Refer to: *The Driving Manual*, Section 2, page 39.

To survive in today's congested traffic conditions and complex road systems, you need to learn to drive defensively. This means that you should be making sure, as far as you can, that you, your passengers and all other road users around you are not put at risk.

You need to be aware that not everyone else on the road will drive according to the rules. You will have to take their actions into account and make allowances for them when they do something wrong.

This is called 'defensive driving'. It means that whatever the circumstances, you will arrive safely at your destination!

No matter how well you drive, accidents are likely to happen! Whether or not you are involved yourself, if you arrive at the scene of an accident it is important that you understand basic safety procedures. You may be able to offer some help which could save someone's life.

It is therefore important that, as a driver, you take the responsibility of learning the basics about first aid. It is equally important that you know about 'what not to do', as well as 'what to do'. Taking the wrong action can sometimes be as serious as taking no action at all.

You may find it helpful to attend a first-aid course, in which case you should contact your local branch of The St John Ambulance Brigade for further information.

This section tests your understanding of how you can minimise the risk of becoming involved in an accident by driving defensively; and what to do if you are unfortunate enough to be involved in, or arrive at the scene of, an accident.

Before answering the questions in this Section read:

- *Your Driving Test* – Section 7; page: 38.
- *The Highway Code* – rules: 48, 107, 113, 127, 128, 136, 150, 153, 154 and 230; pages: 53, 66, 70, 75, 76 and 94; point 90
- *The Driving Manual* – pages: 45, 46, 68, 89, 138, 154, 158, 160, 161, 163, 165, 168, 262, 263, 267, 269, 270 and 307.
- *Learn to Drive in 10 Easy Stages* – pages: 37, 135 and 165.

⊙QUESTIONS⊙

Remember to select only one answer unless indicated otherwise.

1. **After you have passed your test, you can improve your driving by:**

   (a) Buying a better car. ❏
   (b) Practising driving faster. ❏
   (c) Taking a course of Pass-Plus lessons. ❏
   (d) By driving for longer periods. ❏

2. **If you break down on a two-lane road and you have a red warning triangle, you should place this:**

   (a) At least 50 metres to the rear, and on the same side of the road as your car. ❏
   (b) At least 100 metres to the rear, and on the same side of the road as your car. ❏
   (c) On the opposite side of the road to warn oncoming traffic. ❏
   (d) On your open boot lid so that approaching drivers can see it. ❏

3. **If you break down on a motorway, at what distance from the rear of your vehicle should you place a red warning triangle?**

   (a) 50 metres. ❏
   (b) 75 metres. ❏
   (c) 100 metres. ❏
   (d) 150 metres. ❏

4. **If you are involved in an accident involving damage only to vehicles or property, you are required by law to:**

   (a) Exchange names, addresses and insurance details. ❏
   (b) Report the accident to the police within 24 hours. ❏
   (c) Give your driving licence number to the other driver. ❏
   (d) Give your name and vehicle registration number to witnesses. ❏

5. **Telephone marker posts on motorways are spaced:**

   (a) 100 yards apart. ❏
   (b) 100 metres apart. ❏
   (c) 150 yards apart. ❏
   (d) 150 metres apart. ❏

6. **Motorway telephones are connected to:**

   (a) The Department of Transport Headquarters. ❏
   (b) The Automobile Association. ❏
   (c) The Royal Automobile Club. ❏
   (d) A police control point. ❏

7. **If you break down on a motorway and cannot get to a service area, should you:**

   (a) Try to get your car off the road and onto the grass bank. ❏
   (b) Stop in the lane you are in and put your red triangle behind. ❏
   (c) Stop in the left-hand lane so as not to obstruct overtaking traffic. ❏
   (d) Try to get your car onto the hard shoulder as soon as you realise you have a problem. ❏

8. **You are involved in an accident in which one of your passengers is slightly injured. You do not have your insurance documents with you. You will need to report the accident to the police:**

   (a) If your insurance company asks you to. ❏
   (b) As soon as possible, but within 24 hours. ❏
   (c) Within 48 hours. ❏
   (d) Within 7 days. ❏

9. **You stop to give assistance at the scene of an accident involving a goods vehicle. You notice that the lorry is carrying a plain orange reflectorised plate. This means that the vehicle:**

   (a) Is on Ministry of Defence work. ❏
   (b) Carries dangerous goods in packages. ❏
   (c) Is on an international journey. ❏
   (d) Is being used for motorway maintenance. ❏

10. **You are involved in an accident on a level crossing and your vehicle breaks down. Should you first:**

   (a) Try to push the car off the crossing. ❏
   (b) Phone the signal operator. ❏
   (c) Walk along the line to warn any approaching train drivers. ❏
   (d) Get your passengers out of the car and clear of the crossing. ❏

11. Defensive driving is based on:

(a) Driving more slowly so as to avoid accidents. ☐
(b) Effective observations, good anticipation and control. ☐
(c) Skilful control of the car at high speeds. ☐
(d) Using a car with better safety features. ☐

12. You should always drive at a speed:

(a) At which you can stop safely within the distance you can see to be clear. ☐
(b) So that you are able to overtake when necessary. ☐
(c) So that you keep well ahead of the following vehicle. ☐
(d) Which is no more than 10 mph above the speed limit. ☐

13. Motorcycles are often involved in accidents with cars pulling out of junctions because:

(a) They are going too fast. ☐
(b) They are often less easy to notice. ☐
(c) They are generally used by young riders. ☐
(d) Their riders are not taught properly. ☐

14. **You are following a slower moving car along a two-lane road which has a 60 mph speed limit. There are some dips in the road ahead, but you cannot see any approaching traffic. Would you:**

    (a) Overtake before you reach the first dip. ❏

    (b) Wait until you can see far enough ahead to be absolutely ❏ positive there is nothing coming the other way.

    (c) Flash your headlights to warn any oncoming drivers ❏ that you are about to overtake.

    (d) Not overtake, even though there are some long straight ❏ stretches of road with broken centre line markings.

15. **Reading the road ahead helps you to:**
    (Select two answers)

    (a) Avoid tunnel vision. ❏

    (b) Use your mirrors frequently. ❏

    (c) Be more proficient at reading maps. ❏

    (d) Anticipate what might happen. ❏

16. You are on a two-lane dual carriageway approaching a round-about at which you are going straight ahead. Because there is a heavy slow-moving lorry in the left-hand lane ahead, you have positioned in the right-hand lane. The lorry moves away before you reach the junction and you can see that there is no traffic approaching from the right. Should you:

(a) Continue and try to accelerate past the lorry. ❏
(b) Proceed into the roundabout and follow the lorry into ❏
the left-hand lane in the new road.
(c) Move into the roundabout, but hold back, allowing for ❏
the lorry to move across into your lane.
(d) Wait at the 'Give Way' line until the lorry has left the ❏
roundabout.

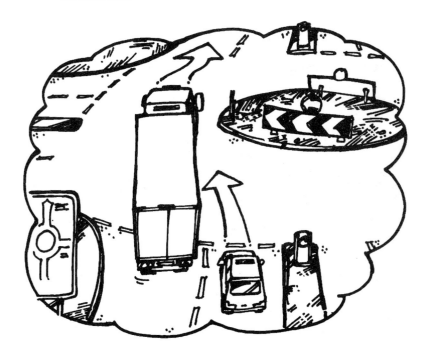

17. Driving along, you notice a sign for a crossroads. You have priority as the roads to the left and right are marked with 'Give Way' lines. You see a car approaching the junction to your left at high speed. Should you:

   (a) Keep going at the same speed because it's your right of way. ☐

   (b) Sound your horn as you pass the other driver. ☐

   (c) Check your mirrors and slow down in case the car keeps coming. ☐

   (d) Accelerate quickly through the junction to avoid the danger. ☐

18. When parking your vehicle in a busy car park you should always try to park:

   (a) At the end of a row. ☐

   (b) By driving in forwards. ☐

   (c) By reversing into the space. ☐

   (d) In a double space to make it easier to manoeuvre. ☐

19. Before you move off from the side of the road you should:

   (a) Check all of your mirrors, give a signal and go. ☐

   (b) Check the interior and offside door mirrors, signal and go. ☐

   (c) Check all of the mirrors, give a signal if necessary and go. ☐

   (d) Check all of the mirrors, give a signal if necessary, check the blind areas and go if safe. ☐

20. As a means of promoting road safety through improved driving standards, the DSA regularly use a slogan which gives drivers a particular aim. This is:

   (a) Safety First. ☐

   (b) If You Drink – Don't Drive. ☐

   (c) Drive Safely – Pass Your Test. ☐

   (d) Safe Driving for Life. ☐

21. **If you break down on a motorway and you need to use one of the emergency phones, you should make a special mention to the operator if you are:**

    (a) A goods vehicle driver. ❏
    (b) A learner driver. ❏
    (c) An express delivery driver. ❏
    (d) A woman travelling alone. ❏

22. **You are the first to arrive at the scene of an accident and need to attend to an injured person. What can you give them to drink?**

    (a) Cold water. ❏
    (b) Whisky or brandy. ❏
    (c) Hot, sweet tea. ❏
    (d) Nothing. ❏

23. **You are driving along in the right-hand lane of a dual carriageway at roughly the same speed as the traffic in the left lane. Where should you not stay for too long?**

    (a) In another driver's blind spot. ❏
    (b) Behind the other vehicle. ❏
    (c) Alongside the other vehicle. ❏
    (d) In front of the other vehicle. ❏

24. **You are allowed to enter a box junction only when you can see that your exit road is clear. You can wait in the area of yellow criss-cross lines when:**

    (a) Traffic is congested and moving very slowly. ❏
    (b) You are turning left and you are held up by pedestrians crossing the road. ❏
    (c) You are turning right and are prevented from doing so by oncoming traffic. ❏
    (d) When you would hold up other traffic wanting to turn left. ❏

25. **You are one of the first to arrive at the scene of an accident. Your first priority should be to:**

   (a) Drive to a phone to summon help. ☐

   (b) Warn other drivers by displaying a red warning triangle ☐ or by using some other device.

   (c) Get any uninjured passengers to a place of safety away ☐ from the vehicles involved.

   (d) Remove any casualties from danger. ☐

26. **The dangers immediately after a road accident are: (Select three answers)**

   (a) Further collisions. ☐

   (b) The speed of approaching emergency vehicles. ☐

   (c) The vulnerability of victims and helpers. ☐

   (d) Fire. ☐

27. **If you are the first to arrive at the scene of an accident, you should:**
(Select three answers)

(a) Move all casualties out of vehicles. ❑
(b) Block the road off completely. ❑
(c) Impose a 'no smoking' ban. ❑
(d) Switch off engines. ❑
(e) Get someone to call the emergency vehicles. ❑

28. **If an accident victim's breathing stops, you should:**

(a) Remove any belts being worn. ❑
(c) Tilt their head backwards. ❑
(d) Tilt their head forwards. ❑
(d) Do not move the head at all. ❑

29. **If a casualty has a leg injury which is bleeding badly, you should:**
(Select two answers)

(a) Ring for the blood transfusion service. ❑
(b) Lower the limb, unless it is broken. ❑
(c) Apply firm pressure over the wound. ❑
(d) Raise the limb to lessen the bleeding. ❑

30. **If a vehicle carrying dangerous goods is involved in an accident, you should immediately ensure that:**
(Select three answers)

(a) Engines are switched off. ❑
(b) A no smoking ban is imposed. ❑
(c) Emergency services are informed about the substances. ❑
(d) You leave the scene immediately. ❑

⟨∘ANSWERS∘⟩

1. **The correct answer is (c).**

   Driving a better car will not improve your driving skills. Practising at driving faster may mean you put yourself at greater risk because of your inexperience. Driving for long periods can make you tired and you may lose your concentration.

   It is a good idea to improve your driving skills in a wider variety of situations with your driving instructor under the Pass-Plus scheme.

   Refer to: *Your Driving Test*, Section 7; ask your driving instructor for more information.

2. **The correct answer is (a).**

   Placing the warning triangle 50 metres behind and on the same side as the obstruction should give approaching drivers adequate warning. They are more at risk from the obstruction than drivers approaching from the opposite direction. Placing the triangle in the rear window or inside an open boot lid would obviously have very little effect as it is unlikely to be seen.

   Refer to: *The Highway Code*, rule 150; *The Driving Manual*, Section 14, page 262; *Learn to Drive in 10 Easy Stages*, Stage 9, page 165.

3. **The correct answer is (d).**

   On a motorway the red triangle should be placed at least 150 metres before the obstruction. Because of the higher speeds this greater distance gives drivers earlier warning of the hazard. Try to get your vehicle as far over to the left as you can, away from danger.

   Refer to: *The Highway Code*, rule 150.

4. **The correct answer is (a).**

   In an accident which only involves damage to vehicles, you should exchange names, addresses and insurance details with the other driver or the owner of the property which has been damaged. As long as you give these details, you do not necessarily need to report the accident to the police.

   Refer to: *The Highway Code*, page 70.

5. **The correct answer is (b).**

   Motorway telephone marker posts are spaced at intervals of 100 metres (110 yards). They show you the direction of the nearest telephone point. The telephones are spaced at one mile intervals so that you should not need to walk further than half a mile to one. You should never cross the carriageway to reach a phone. This is dangerous, illegal and pointless as they are always situated directly opposite each other on the carriageways.
   Refer to: *The Driving Manual,* Section 14, page 263.

6. **The correct answer is (d).**

   Motorway telephones are connected to a police control point. The police will send out a breakdown vehicle or call one of the national services such as the AA, RAC or National Breakdown to send a vehicle to you. It is clearly an advantage to belong to one of these services as the cost of being towed off a motorway for repairs can be extremely expensive.
   Refer to: *The Driving Manual,* Section 14, page 263.

7. **The correct answer is (d).**

   If you realise there is something wrong with your car, you should try to get to a service area. However, if this is not possible, you need to get the car off the carriageway and onto the hard shoulder. Signal your intentions and move over safely and without braking harshly. Get as far to the left as possible on the hard shoulder and switch on your hazard warning lights.
   Refer to: *The Driving Manual,* Section 14, page 263.

8. **The correct answer is (b).**

   If anyone is injured in an accident and you are unable to produce your insurance details at the time, you must report the accident to the police as soon as possible, and at least within 24 hours.
   Refer to: *The Highway Code,* page 70.

9. **The correct answer is (b).**

Vehicles carrying potentially dangerous goods in packages are often marked with the rectangular plates which are illustrated on page 66 of *The Highway Code*. It is important that you know what these plates mean.
Refer to: *The Highway Code*, rule 154.

10. **The correct answer is (d).**

If you have an accident, or your vehicle breaks down on a level crossing, the first thing to do is get your passengers out and into a place of safety. Only then should you consider whether to contact the signal operator and/or try to move the vehicle clear of the crossing.
Refer to: *The Highway Code*, rule 230.

11. **The correct answer is (b).**

Driving defensively means keeping you, your passengers, your car and other road users out of danger. This involves awareness, planning well ahead, anticipating and staying in control. It means that you should drive with care, responsibility, consideration and courtesy.
Refer to: *The Driving Manual*, Section 8, page 158.

12. **The correct answer is (a).**

Never drive beyond the limits of your vision. When you are approaching a bend, for example, your main consideration should be your lack of vision around the bend, and whether you would be able to stop safely if there was an obstruction just out of sight. The fact that your car might get round the bend at a higher speed is not relevant.
Refer to: *The Driving Manual*, Section 8, page 160.

13. **The correct answer is (b).**

Motorcycles take up a lot less space on the road compared with cars and other vehicles. They are, therefore, less easy to see. Motorcycles and bicycles may be travelling far faster than they appear to be.
Refer to: *The Driving Manual*, Section 8, page 161.

14. The correct answer is (b).

Don't be impatient! An area of the road which is hidden in hollows is called 'dead ground'. You could end up dead if you overtake when you can't see! Solid white lines in the centre of the road will warn you of the danger. If there is someone in the dip coming the other way, flashing your lights will not help – particularly if it's daylight and the lights can't be seen!

Be patient! Wait until there is a stretch of the road where you can see far enough and, if you have sufficient time and there are no solid white lines, be prepared to make progress and go. However, do not be prepared to take any risks.

Refer to: *The Driving Manual*, Section 5, page 89.

15. The correct answers are (b) and (d).

Reading the road ahead will help you to anticipate what might happen well in advance. The earlier you spot a problem the sooner you can be checking your mirrors so that you are able to let following drivers know what you are doing. This is part of 'defensive driving'.

Tunnel vision is a physical problem and will not be helped by just looking ahead.

Refer to: *The Driving Manual*, Section 3, page 45; Section 8, page 163.

16. The correct answer is (c).

Trying to accelerate past the lorry may put you in danger as it could take an unusual course through the roundabout. Waiting for it to clear the roundabout and then following it into the left lane will probably result in your becoming boxed in behind it. Waiting at the 'Give Way' line when you can see there is nothing approaching from the right may be showing unnecessary caution – particularly if a driver behind thinks you are going to keep moving!

The sensible thing to do would be to proceed into the space in the roundabout to make progress and stay in the right-hand lane. Hold back to allow for the unusual course the lorry may be taking. This will also mean that you will not be in the lorry driver's blind area.

Refer to: *Your Driving Test*, page 38; *The Highway Code*, rules 127 and 128; *The Driving Manual*, Section 6, page 138; Section 8, page 168; *Learn to Drive in 10 Easy Stages*, Stage 8, page 135.

17. The correct answer is (c).

It could be dangerous to assume that other drivers will always apply the rules. Although you may have priority, it is unsafe to proceed thinking 'It is my right of way'. Sounding the horn as you drive past is of little use if the driver has already decided to pull out. Accelerating out of this potentially dangerous situation means you could be accelerating into another!

Refer to: *Your Driving Test*, page 38; *The Highway Code*, rules 107 and 136; *The Driving Manual*, Section 5, page 68; Section 8, page 165.

18. The correct answer is (c).

It is nearly always best to reverse into parking spaces. It makes it easier and safer to get out because you will have a better view, especially at night or if you have back seat passengers. If you drive forwards into the space, you will find that it may take several movements to and fro to get into a satisfactory position in the middle of the parking bay. You certainly should not be taking up two parking spaces. Not only is this selfish, but in some car parks you could be wheel-clamped .

Refer to: *The Driving Manual*, Section 7, page 154.

19. The correct answer is (d).

Never assume it is safe to move off unless you have checked all around. Use all of your mirrors and decide whether or not you need to signal. When there is a safe space to move into, take a final check of the blind area to make sure no one is there. Move off only if you are sure you will not inconvenience or endanger any other road user. If in doubt – WAIT!

Refer to: *Learn to Drive in 10 Easy Stages*, Stage 3, page 37; *Your Driving Test*, page 17; *The Highway Code*, rule 48; *The Driving Manual*, Section 3, pages 45 and 46.

20. The correct answer is (d).

'Safe Driving for Life' should be the aim of all drivers. This means much more than just passing the Test or improving your practical skills or obeying the basic rules. It involves knowing all about defensive driving techniques and developing safe, positive attitudes.

Refer to: *The Driving Manual*, 'Introduction', and also page 323.

21. The correct answer is (d).

Women travelling alone are particularly vulnerable. The emergency services and breakdown operators give them priority and try to get assistance to them at the earliest opportunity. While you are using the emergency phone make sure that you face the oncoming traffic and after using the phone wait on the grass bank near your vehicle. In this way you will be safer than if waiting in your vehicle and you will see the approaching emergency vehicle in your mirrors. Some motorway accidents involve vehicles running into people and vehicles on the hard shoulder.

Refer to: *The Driving Manual*, Section 9, page 197.

22. The correct answer is (d).

You do not know what internal injuries may have been sustained.

Refer to: *The Highway Code*, page 76.

23. The correct answer is (a).

To drive defensively and with consideration you should always try to avoid staying in another driver's blind spot for longer than is necessary. This is particularly important when larger vehicles are involved and when you are travelling on multi-laned roads.

Try to adjust your speed and position so that you are a little further forward or back so that the driver is able to see your vehicle either in the mirrors or out of the side windows. You can often achieve this by making sure that you can see the other driver's eyes in their mirrors.

Refer to: *The Driving Manual*, Section 3, page 47.

24. The correct answer is (c).

The criss-cross yellow lines painted on the road at some junctions are intended to keep traffic flowing. You should not enter this area unless you can see that your exit is clear. You are, however, allowed to wait in the box if you are turning right and you are only prevented from doing so by oncoming traffic.

Refer to: *The Highway Code*, rule 113; *The Driving Manual*, Section 19, page 307.

25. The correct answer is (b).

If you are one of the first to arrive at the scene of an accident you need to make sure that other traffic has some sort of warning so as to avoid any further accident. This can be done by the most appropriate means – hazard warning lights, warning triangles, or by organising someone to direct traffic. You can then turn your attention to other priorities – calling the emergency services, moving the uninjured to a safe place, giving first aid and so on.

Refer to: *The Driving Manual*, Section 14, page 267; *The Highway Code*, pages 75 and 76.

26. The correct answers are (a), (c) and (d).

Further collisions can and do happen – be aware of this and try to warn others. Both the victims and helpers can become involved in any of the dangers. Fire is a major hazard, particularly if there are any fuel leakages. The emergency vehicles will be approaching at speed, however they will slow down nearing the scene of the accident.

Refer to: *The Driving Manual*, Section 14, page 267; *The Highway Code*, pages 75, 94, point 90.

27. The correct answers are (c), (d) and (e).

You should not move casualties trapped in vehicles unless they are in danger because you could cause more injury. Blocking off the road completely might cause problems for the emergency vehicles and in any case, it may be possible to keep the road open for other traffic. Engines should be switched off and a 'no smoking' ban imposed because of the risk of fire. If it has not already been done someone should be directed to call the emergency services.

Refer to: *The Driving Manual*, Section 14, page 267.

28. The correct answers are (a), (b) and (c).

Serious injury could be caused by trying to remove a crash helmet – unless it is essential. The airways must be kept open by tilting the head backwards. Obstructions which could prevent breathing should be removed from the mouth.

Refer to: *The Driving Manual*, Section 14, page 269.

29. The correct answers are (c) and (d).

Lowering a badly bleeding limb will cause more bleeding. Raising the limb will slow down the blood flow. Applying firm pressure will have a similar effect. Casualties should be given nothing to eat or drink.

Refer to: *The Driving Manual*, Section 14, page 270.

30. The correct answers are (a), (b) and (c).

Normal accident procedure should be followed, which includes switching off engines and imposing a 'no smoking' ban. Give as much information as possible about the substances to the emergency services. This will help them deal with any spillages. If you are the only person around, don't just leave the scene!

Refer to: *The Highway Code*, rules 153 and 154.

PROGRESS CHART FOR THEORY TEST KNOWLEDGE

Section Attempted	First Attempt SCORE	Second Attempt SCORE	Third Attempt SCORE
1. Legal Requirements	◯	◯	◯
2. Safety Equipment	◯	◯	◯
3. Rules of the Road	◯	◯	◯
4. Following and Stopping Distances	◯	◯	◯
5. Effects of Alcohol, Drugs etc	◯	◯	◯
6. Forward Planning, Hazard Perception and Safe Attitudes	◯	◯	◯
7. Vehicle Characteristics	◯	◯	◯
8. Mechanical Principles and Fault Detection	◯	◯	◯
9. Vehicle Security and Environmental Issues	◯	◯	◯
10. Defensive Driving and Accident Procedure	◯	◯	◯
TOTALS SCORED	◯	◯	◯

MOCK TESTS

Remember, when you take your Theory Test you have to score 30 out of 35. If you have achieved a score of at least 28 out of the 30 questions in each of the previous sections of this book, and you have read all of the other recommended materials, you should have no trouble with these two 'Mock Test' papers.

If you get any of the answers wrong, then go back and read those subjects which you did not know. If you have any difficulty in understanding anything, ask your driving instructor.

Remember, select only one answer unless otherwise indicated.

MOCK TEST 1

1. **If your car has front fog lights, you should switch them on when:**

   (a) Other drivers have switched theirs on. ❑
   (b) You are driving on country roads. ❑
   (c) When visibility falls below 100 metres. ❑
   (d) As soon as it gets dark. ❑

2. **The maximum safe speed at which to drive is dictated by: (Select two answers)**

   (a) The road and weather conditions. ❑
   (b) The speed limit signs. ❑
   (c) The amount of pedestrian activity. ❑
   (d) The speed of the other traffic. ❑

3. **When filling up at a service station, you should always: (Select two answers)**

   (a) Not smoke. ❑
   (b) Switch off your engine. ❑
   (c) Check your tyre pressure. ❑
   (d) Check your oil level. ❑

4. **A 'clearway' sign means:**

   (a) End of speed limit restrictions. ❑
   (b) The national speed limit applies. ❑
   (c) Waiting restrictions apply. ❑
   (d) No stopping on the carriageway. ❑

5. **When turning right at crossroads where an oncoming vehicle is also turning right, you may:**
   (Select two answers)

   (a) Stop and wave the other driver across. ❏
   (b) Turn offside to offside, passing behind the other vehicle. ❏
   (c) Turn nearside to nearside, crossing the front of it. ❏
   (d) Take the shortest line across the junction as soon as you possibly can. ❏

6. **A circular sign with a blue background gives:**

   (a) A warning. ❏
   (b) A positive instruction. ❏
   (c) Directions. ❏
   (d) Motorway information. ❏

7. **When you see any triangular sign, you should:**

   (a) Slow down and stop. ❏
   (b) Give way to traffic on the major road. ❏
   (c) Watch out for pedestrians in the road. ❏
   (d) Check your mirrors, adjust your speed and allow for a hazard ahead. ❏

8. **When turning at junctions, you should take particular care in looking out for:**
    (Select three answers)

    (a) Motorcyclists. ❑
    (b) Cyclists. ❑
    (c) Pedestrians. ❑
    (d) Speed limit signs. ❑

9. **If you are towing a caravan and it begins 'snaking' from side to side, you should:**

    (a) Brake hard to stop quickly. ❑
    (b) Slow down gradually. ❑
    (c) Increase your speed to stop the snaking. ❑
    (d) Let the steering wheel centre itself to stop the snaking. ❑

10. **Arm signals can be useful to other road users. They should be considered when:**
    (Select three answers)

    (a) Turning at all junctions. ❑
    (b) Your indicators may be difficult to see in bright sunlight. ❑
    (c) Stopping at pedestrian crossings. ❑
    (d) Turning off a major road into property. ❑

11. **A 'STOP' sign and solid white line are usually found at junctions which:**

    (a) Lead into high streets. ❑
    (b) Are particularly busy. ❑
    (c) Have poor visibility into the major road. ❑
    (d) Lead on to bus routes. ❑

12. **First gear in a car is the:**

    (a) Most powerful. ❑
    (b) Most economical. ❑
    (c) Least powerful. ❑
    (d) Fastest. ❑

13. Interior mirrors should be:

(a) Biassed towards the nearside. ❏
(b) Adjusted to give a clear view to the rear. ❏
(c) Biassed to the offside. ❏
(d) Adjusted to see your left ear in the corner of it. ❏

14. Road humps are:
(Select two answers)

(a) Designed to be driven over at only 25 – 30 mph. ❏
(b) Used to reduce the speed of all traffic. ❏
(c) Designed to be driven over at very low speeds. ❏
(d) Used to control the speed of goods traffic in built-up ❏
    areas.

15. If you have a full driving licence for Category B (the licence you need for driving a car), you may:
(Select two answers)

(a) Ride a moped. ❏
(b) Drive a light goods vehicle up to 3.5 tonnes. ❏
(c) Drive a minibus with between 9 and 12 seats. ❏
(d) Drive or ride any vehicle up to 7.5 tonnes. ❏

16. How long must you have held a full driving licence before you can supervise a learner driver?

(a) Six months. ❏
(b) One year. ❏
(c) Two years. ❏
(d) Three years. ❏

17. What would you use a jack for?

(a) Replacing a spark plug. ❏
(b) Testing the battery power. ❏
(c) Changing a wheel. ❏
(d) Checking fan belt tension ❏

18. **When driving a high performance car on a motorway, you should:**

    (a) Always keep to the left lane except when overtaking. ❏
    (b) Stay in the middle lane to avoid too many lane changes. ❏
    (c) Drive in the right-hand lane to make overtaking easier. ❏
    (d) Overtake on either side only when it is safe to do so. ❏

19. **The right-hand lane on a three-laned dual motorway may not be used by:**
    (Select three answers)

    (a) Vehicles travelling at less than 70 mph. ❏
    (b) Large goods vehicles over 7.5 tonnes. ❏
    (c) Any bus or coach longer than 12 metres. ❏
    (d) Cars towing caravans. ❏

20. **On right-hand bends you should position to the:**
    (Select two answers)

    (a) Left to improve your view. ❏
    (b) Right so you will be seen by oncoming drivers. ❏
    (c) Left to avoid oncoming drivers. ❏
    (d) Right to enable you to keep your speed up. ❏

21. **If a vehicle pulls out of a junction into your path, you should:**

    (a) Slow down and hold back to allow it to get clear. ❏
    (b) Drive up close behind so the driver knows you are there. ❏
    (c) Flash your lights to warn the driver of your presence. ❏
    (d) Overtake as soon as possible and then slow down. ❏

22. **If a following driver is trying to overtake you, you should:**
    (Select two answers)

    (a) Wave the other driver by. ❏
    (b) Keep to a steady course. ❏
    (c) Accelerate so as not to slow down the other driver. ❏
    (d) Pull over if safe and allow the other driver to pass. ❏

23. You may cross a double white line:
(Select two answers)

(a) To enter or leave property. ❏

(b) When directed to do so by a police officer in uniform. ❏

(c) To pass a pedal cyclist travelling at 15–20 mph. ❏

(d) To overtake any vehicle if it is safe. ❏

24. Where there is an area of road marked with white diagonal stripes and bordered with an unbroken white line, you must:

(a) Enter it only if you can see that it is safe. ❏

(b) Never enter it. ❏

(c) Only enter it in an emergency. ❏

(d) Enter it only when turning right. ❏

25. You will see green coloured reflecting road studs:

(a) Marking the central reserve on motorways. ❏

(b) In between the lanes on dual carriageways. ❏

(c) Marking the left edge of the road. ❏

(d) Across lay-bys and side roads. ❏

26. The zig-zag lines at pedestrian crossings mean:
(Select two answers)

(a) No stopping. ❏

(b) No parking. ❏

(c) No overtaking. ❏

(d) Pedestrians have right of way. ❏

27. If the oil warning light comes on while you are driving you should:

(a) Drive to the nearest garage as quickly as possible. ❏

(b) Stop and investigate the problem immediately. ❏

(c) Check the oil as soon as you get home. ❏

(d) Switch off the engine, let it cool down and then continue. ❏

28. If you are first to arrive at the scene of a road accident you should:
(Select two answers)

(a) Move any casualties away from the scene. ❏

(b) Warn other traffic. ❏

(c) Make sure engines are switched off. ❏

(d) Give the injured a warm drink if available. ❏

29. This road sign means:

    (a) Dual carriageway ahead. ☐

    (b) Use the hard shoulder. ☐

    (c) Pass either side. ☐

    (d) End of motorway restrictions. ☐

30. Dipped headlights should be used:
(Select three answers)

    (a) When they will help others see you. ☐

    (b) At night on all roads without street lighting. ☐

    (c) Where the street lights are less than 185 metres apart. ☐

    (d) Whenever visibility is seriously reduced. ☐

31. Signs giving orders are mostly:

    (a) Blue circles. ☐

    (b) Red circles. ☐

    (c) Blue triangles. ☐

    (d) Red triangles. ☐

32. What does this traffic sign mean?

    (a) Farm entrance. ☐

    (b) Level crossing with no barrier or gate. ☐

    (c) Level crossing with barrier or gate. ☐

    (d) Private road. ☐

33. The background colour of signs for tourist attractions is normally:

    (a) Blue. ❏
    (b) Brown. ❏
    (c) Green. ❏
    (d) Yellow. ❏

34. If you have to drive on snow, you should:
    (Select three answers)

    (a) Move away in as high a gear as possible. ❏
    (b) Leave your braking until as late as possible. ❏
    (c) Try to keep moving slowly when travelling up hills. ❏
    (d) Use all of the controls gradually and smoothly. ❏

35. If you have been drinking heavily at a party and take a taxi home, the following morning you:
    (Select two answers)

    (a) Will legally be all right to drive your car home. ❏
    (b) May still be over the legally allowed limit for driving. ❏
    (c) May drive your car but should stay on quiet roads. ❏
    (d) Would be safer asking someone else to drive your car. ❏

MOCK TEST 2

1. What is the minimum age at which a driver may legally supervise a learner?

    (a) 17 years. ❏
    (b) 18 years. ❏
    (c) 20 years. ❏
    (d) 21 years. ❏

2. When drivers reach the age of 70, they have to renew their driving licence. The new licence for a person with no medical conditions will be valid for:

    (a) One year. ❏
    (b) Three years. ❏
    (c) Five years. ❏
    (d) Ten years. ❏

3. **The Highway Code states that signals should be given:**
   (Select two answers)

   (a) Always when moving off. ❑
   (b) To help and warn other road users. ❑
   (c) Always when stopping. ❑
   (d) Clearly and in plenty of time. ❑

4. **If you are travelling at 40 mph in good conditions, the overall stopping distance is:**

   (a) 12 metres (40 feet). ❑
   (b) 23 metres (75 feet). ❑
   (c) 36 metres (120 feet). ❑
   (d) 53 metres (175 feet). ❑

5. **If there is a police car behind you and the police want you to stop your vehicle they will:**
   (Select three answers)

   (a) Flash their headlights or blue light. ❑
   (b) Sound their horn or siren. ❑
   (c) Point to the left and use the left indicator. ❑
   (d) Use their hazard warning lights. ❑

6. **When driving on multi-laned roads, you should always maintain good lane discipline. Before changing lanes you should, first of all:**

   (a) Switch on your indicator to let others know your intentions. ❑
   (b) Change to a lower gear to give you more power. ❑
   (c) Check the mirrors to make sure you won't affect anyone. ❑
   (d) Start moving over to confirm your intentions. ❑

7. **Badly adjusted headlights can:**
   (Select two answers)

   (a) Help others see you earlier. ❑
   (b) Dazzle others. ❑
   (c) Cause accidents. ❑
   (d) Cause the bulbs to fuse. ❑

8. **When driving on wet roads you should remember:**
   (Select two answers)

   (a) The grip of the tyres on the surface will be reduced. ❏
   (b) You will need more braking distance. ❏
   (c) You will need to keep less than two seconds behind the ❏
       vehicle in front.
   (d) You will skid on certain types of road surface. ❏

9. **If you are driving at speed and suddenly find yourself sliding**
   forwards on a thin film of water, you are more likely to aqua-
   plane if you:
   (Select two answers)

   (a) Slow down by easing off the accelerator. ❏
   (b) Brake or try to change direction. ❏
   (c) Don't allow at least double the normal braking distance. ❏
   (d) Have only recently had new tyres fitted. ❏

10. **Third party insurance is the minimum cover required by law.**
    This covers you for:
    (Select two answers)

    (a) Injury to any third party. ❏
    (b) Damage to a third party's property. ❏
    (c) Damage only to your vehicle. ❏
    (d) Theft of your vehicle. ❏

11. **If you buy a second-hand vehicle you should be given the vehi-**
    cle registration document. This contains a 'change of owner-
    ship' section and you must:
    (Select two answers)

    (a) Fill in the change of ownership details. ❏
    (b) Hand this back to the person who sold you the vehicle. ❏
    (c) Keep this in a safe place until you sell the vehicle. ❏
    (d) Send it to the DVLA immediately. ❏

12. **All road vehicles must have a road tax disc on display. When you sell your car you:**
    (Select two answers)

    (a) May apply for a refund for any remaining period on ❏
       the disc.
    (b) May transfer the disc to your new vehicle. ❏
    (c) May not transfer the disc to any other vehicle. ❏
    (d) Will lose all the remaining period on the disc. ❏

13. **The speed limit for a car towing a caravan on a single-carriage-way road outside a built-up area is:**

    (a) 40 mph. ❏
    (b) 45 mph. ❏
    (c) 50 mph. ❏
    (d) 55 mph. ❏

14. **You should dip your headlights:**
    (Select two answers)

    (a) Earlier when approaching left-hand bends. ❏
    (b) Earlier when approaching right-hand bends. ❏
    (c) Early enough to avoid dazzling oncoming drivers. ❏
    (d) Later if an oncoming driver keeps full beam on. ❏

15. **If you find yourself faced with an emergency situation, you should:**

    (a) Push down the clutch first and then brake. ❏
    (b) Use the brake and clutch at the same time. ❏
    (c) Brake as hard as you can. ❏
    (d) Brake firmly and progressively, then push down the ❏
       clutch.

16. **When turning left from a minor into a major road, you should:**

    (a) Keep looking to the left where you're going. ❏
    (b) Look left, right and left again. ❏
    (c) Look right, left and then right again. ❏
    (d) Take effective observation before emerging. ❏

17. When you are travelling at night you should be able to stop:
(Select two answers)

    (a) Well within the braking distance. ❏
    (b) Within the range of your lights. ❏
    (c) Within the distance you can see is clear. ❏
    (d) More quickly than in daylight. ❏

18. If you have to park at night on a road which has a 40 mph speed limit, you should:
(Select three answers)

    (a) Park at least ten metres away from any junction. ❏
    (b) Leave on your sidelights. ❏
    (c) Park facing the direction of the traffic flow. ❏
    (d) Park facing against the direction of the traffic flow. ❏

19. Defensive driving means:
(Select two answers)

    (a) Always driving as slowly as possible. ❏
    (b) Always driving up to the speed limit. ❏
    (c) Never assuming that other drivers will follow the rules. ❏
    (d) Always making allowances for other drivers' mistakes. ❏

20. When following other vehicles on a dry road in heavy slow-moving urban traffic, the minimum distance you should maintain is:

    (a) The thinking distance. ❏
    (b) The braking distance. ❏
    (c) The overall stopping distance. ❏
    (d) A two-second gap. ❏

21. Multiple collisions often happen because drivers:
(Select three answers)

    (a) Do not allow sufficient room between themselves and the vehicle in front. ❏
    (b) Often exceed the speed limits. ❏
    (c) Are unable to brake in time. ❏
    (d) Are not looking far enough ahead. ❏

22. **If you are travelling downhill and there is an obstruction on your side of the road, be prepared to:**
(Select two answers)

   (a) Accelerate to get past before oncoming vehicles reach the obstruction. ❏

   (b) Brake earlier than usual when giving way. ❏

   (c) Give way when necessary, as oncoming vehicles have priority. ❏

   (d) Expect those coming up the hill to give way to you because it's more difficult for you to brake downhill. ❏

23. **If traffic lights are not working, you should:**
(Select two answers)

   (a) Try to get through quickly to avoid conflict with others. ❏

   (b) Proceed with great care. ❏

   (c) Treat the junction as if it were unmarked. ❏

   (d) Stop at the line until the lights start working again. ❏

24. **When you take your practical driving test, the driving examiner will be checking to make sure you are using your mirrors correctly. You should:**
(Select three answers)

   (a) Adjust them so you need to move your head to use them. ❏

   (b) Check all of them regularly. ❏

   (c) Act sensibly on what you see. ❏

   (d) Delay a right turn signal if you see someone overtaking you. ❏

25. **The correct safety check sequence when entering a car is:**

   (a) Doors, seat, seatbelt, mirrors, ignition, handbrake. ❏

   (b) Doors, mirrors, seatbelt, seat, neutral/handbrake. ❏

   (c) Doors, seat, seatbelt, mirrors, handbrake/neutral. ❏

   (d) Doors, mirrors, seat, seatbelt, handbrake/neutral. ❏

26. **When turning the car around in the road, you should:**

   (a) Keep the vehicle moving briskly and turn the wheel slowly. ❏

   (b) Start steering before the car moves to ensure you get round in three movements. ❏

   (c) Keep the car moving slowly and turn the wheel briskly. ❏

   (d) Expect others to give you priority. ❏

27. **When you see a hazard, you should first of all:**

   (a) Do nothing and wait until the situation develops further. ❏

   (b) Slow down immediately. ❏

   (c) Check your mirrors to see if there is anyone following you. ❏

   (d) Switch on your hazard warning lights. ❏

28. **When you are slowing down, the following driver should see your brake lights. To let an oncoming driver know that you are stopping at a zebra crossing, you could:**

   (a) Flash your headlights. ❏

   (b) Use an arm signal. ❏

   (c) Switch on your hazard warning lights. ❏

   (d) Start braking later. ❏

29. **The normal routine for approaching any type of hazard is M–S–M. The manoeuvre part is further broken down into P–S–L. What does this mean:**

   (a) Position–speed–look. ❏

   (b) Prepare–Signal–Look. ❏

   (c) Peep–Slow–Look. ❏

   (d) Position–Stop–Look. ❏

30. **In some busy towns, bus lanes are in operation to keep the public transport system moving efficiently. Where you see bus lanes you should:**
   (Select two answers)

   (a) Keep out of them at all times. ❏

   (b) Read the signs for information on when you should keep out of them. ❏

   (c) Drive in them at times other than those stated on the signs. ❏

   (d) Stay off these routes altogether to avoid congestion. ❏

31. **If you are approaching a level crossing which is concealed, there may be countdown markers to warn you. These will be:**

    (a) Red bars on a white background. ❑

    (b) White bars on a blue background. ❑

    (c) Yellow bars on a green background. ❑

    (d) White bars on a black background. ❑

32. **Where you see double yellow lines, it means that waiting is prohibited:**
(Select three answers)

    (a) 24 hours a day. ❑

    (b) 7 days a week. ❑

    (c) For at least four consecutive months. ❑

    (d) All year round. ❑

33. **This sign means:**

    (a) Vehicles parked illegally will be towed away. ❑

    (b) Vehicles may park partially on the verge. ❑

    (c) Vehicles must not park on the verge. ❑

    (d) Vehicles may be affected by the adverse camber. ❑

34. This sign means:
(Select two answers)

    (a) Pedestrians in the road for the distance shown. ❏
    (b) Pedestrian crossing ahead, at the distance shown. ❏
    (c) Children going to or from school. ❏
    (d) There is no footway. ❏

35. The Driving Standards Agency motto is:

    (a) 'Drive safely and survive.' ❏
    (b) 'Defensive driving for life.' ❏
    (c) 'Drive safely – live longer.' ❏
    (d) 'Safe driving for life.' ❏

MOCK TEST ANSWERS

Remember, you should aim at scoring at least 30 correct out of the 35 questions. Where you answer incorrectly and don't understand the answers given, ask your instructor for an explanation.

MOCK TEST 1

1. (c)	2. (a) and (c)	3. (a) and (b)	4. (d)
5. (b) and (c)	6. (b)	7. (d)	8. (a), (b) and (c)
9. (b)	10. (b), (c) and (d)	11. (c)	12. (a)
13. (b)	14. (b) and (c)	15. (a) and (b)	16. (d)
17. (c)	18. (a)	19. (b), (c) and (d)	20. (a) and (c)
21. (a)	22. (b) and (d)	23. (a) and (b)	24. (c)
25. (d)	26. (b) and (c)	27. (c)	28. (b) and (c)
29. (b)	30. (a), (b) and (d)	31. (b)	32. (c)
33. (b)	34. (a), (c) and (d)	35. (b) and (d)	

MOCK TEST 2

1. (d)	2. (b)	3. (b) and (d)	4. (c)
5. (a), (b) and (c)	6. (c)	7. (b) and (c)	8. (a) and (b)
9. (b) and (c)	10. (a) and (b)	11. (a) and (d)	12. (a) and (c)
13. (c)	14. (a) and (c)	15. (d)	16. (d)
17. (b) and (c)	18. (a), (b) and (c)	19. (c) and (d)	20. (a)
21. (a), (c) and (d)	22. (b) and (c)	23. (b) and (c)	24. (b), (c) and (d)
25. (c)	26. (c)	27. (c)	28. (b)
29. (a)	30. (b) and (c)	31. (a)	32. (a), (b) and (c)
33. (b)	34 (a) and (d)	35. (d)	

DRIVING
STANDARDS
AGENCY

TT2b   APPLICATION FOR A DRIVING THEORY TEST APPOINTMENT

You can book your Driving Theory Test in one of two ways. **By Post** – Please complete this form and return it to the address below with your cheque or postal order. **By Telephone** – Please ring **0645 000 666** at any time between 8.00 a.m. and 6.00 p.m. Monday to Friday. When you ring please have ready your DVLA Driver Licence Number and credit or debit card details. If you book by telephone we can confirm the date and time of your test immediately. Welsh speakers please ring 0645 700 201. A Minicom machine for the use of candidates with hearing difficulties is available on 0645 700 301.

If you wish to cancel your theory test appointment you must give us at least 3 whole working days' notice or you will forfeit the theory test fee.

Not all learner drivers will need to take a theory test. For example, if you hold a full car licence and are applying for a motorcycle licence, or vice versa, a theory test is not required. This is also the case if you have a full licence to drive a vehicle with automatic transmission and you wish to upgrade your licence to drive vehicles in the same licence category but with manual transmission.

If you have any queries about whether you need a theory test, please telephone the theory test general enquiry number on 0645 000 555.

To take a driving theory test you must have a current GB or Northern Ireland driving licence. **Please bring your licence when you come for your theory test, and make sure you have signed it.** Failure to do so may mean that the test cannot take place and you will lose your test fee.

If, after 2 weeks, you have not received an appointment notification, please contact the theory test booking office immediately. If you miss your appointment you may lose your fee.

PLEASE COMPLETE ALL DETAILS IN CAPITALS AND RETURN TO: DRIVING STANDARDS AGENCY, PO BOX 444, COVENTRY. CV1 2ZY

Driver Licence Number (Copy this from your provisional driving licence)

Type of test	CAR	MOTORCYCLE (incl. Mopeds)	LARGE GOODS (incl. Lorries & Medium Goods)	PASSENGER CARRYING (Buses & Coaches)
(Please ✓ one only)				

Title	First Names	Surname	Date of Birth	Sex
Mr/Mrs/Ms.			Day Month Year	M/F

Address

Please provide contact numbers for use in the event of a query

daytime telephone number   evening telephone number

Postcode

At which centre would you prefer to take the test? (see details overleaf)

What is the earliest preferred date on which you could take a test?

Day   Month   Year

Delete any sessions which you **cannot** attend

Daytime   MON TUE WED THURS FRI SAT

Evening (6 p.m.)   MON TUE WED THURS FRI

Do you require wheelchair access at the test centre? (please delete)   YES / NO

Please let us know if you have any other special needs or any form of reading / writing difficulty e.g. dyslexia, deafness etc. Please provide details below as we may be able to provide assistance for you.

Please indicate if you would like to take a test paper in one of the alternative languages below. (Please ✓)

WELSH   BENGALI   URDU   PUNJABI   CHINESE   GUJERATI   HINDI

Fee enclosed   £

Cheque or Postal Order number

Please write your Driver Licence Number on the back of your cheque or postal order, which should be made payable to "Driving Standards Agency"

I confirm that I hold a provisional licence which entitles me to take this test.

Signature of Candidate

Date

REMEMBER, THE EASIEST WAY TO BOOK IS BY TELEPHONE WITH A CREDIT/DEBIT CARD
IF YOU HAVE ANY QUERIES ON THE APPLICATION FORM OR ABOUT THE DRIVING THEORY TEST,
PLEASE CALL US ON 0645 000 555 OR WRITE TO US AT: DRIVING STANDARDS AGENCY,
PO BOX 444, COVENTRY. CV1 2ZY
In the interest of customer service, your telephone conversation may be recorded.

An executive agency of
THE DEPARTMENT
OF TRANSPORT

GB DRIVING THEORY TEST CENTRES

Written Driving Theory Tests may be taken at any of the following test centres:

Scotland

Borders	Central	Dumfries & Galloway	Fife	Grampian	Highland		
Galashiels	Stirling	Dumfries Stranraer	Dunfermline	Aberdeen Elgin Huntly	Fort William Gairloch Helmsdale Inverness	Isle of Arran Isle of Islay Kyle of Lochalsh Portree	Tongue Ullapool Wick

Lothian	Orkney	Shetland	Tayside	Western Isles	Strathclyde		
Edinburgh	Kirkwall	Lerwick	Dundee Pitlochry	Stornoway Barra Benbecula	Ayr Clydebank Glasgow	Greenock Motherwell Oban	Salen Tarbert

England

Avon	Bedfordshire	Berkshire	Buckinghamshire	Cambridgeshire	Cheshire	Cleveland
Bath Bristol	Luton	Reading Slough	Milton Keynes	Cambridge Peterborough	Chester Runcorn	Middlesbrough

Cornwall	County Durham	Cumbria	Derbyshire	Devon	Dorset	East Sussex
Penzance Truro	Durham	Barrow Carlisle Workington	Chesterfield Derby	Barnstaple Exeter Plymouth Torquay	Bournemouth Weymouth	Brighton Eastbourne Hastings

Essex		Gloucestershire	Greater Manchester		Hampshire	
Basildon Chelmsford Colchester	Harlow Southend-on-Sea	Cheltenham Gloucester	Manchester Oldham Salford	Stockport Wigan	Aldershot Basingstoke Fareham	Portsmouth Southampton

Hereford & Worcester	Hertfordshire	Humberside	Isle of Wight	Kent	Lancashire	
Hereford Worcester	Stevenage Watford	Grimsby Hull Scunthorpe	Newport	Canterbury Gillingham	Blackpool Bolton	Preston Southport

Leicestershire	Lincolnshire	London – Greater		London – Inner	Merseyside	Norfolk
Leicester	Boston Grantham Lincoln	Bexley Croydon Hillingdon	Ilford Kingston Wood Green	Vauxhall	Birkenhead Liverpool St. Helens	Norwich King's Lynn

North Yorkshire	Nothumbria	Northamptonshire	Nottinghamshire	Oxfordshire	Shropshire	Somerset
Harrogate Scarborough York	Morpeth Workington	Northampton	Mansfield Nottingham	Oxford	Shrewsbury	Taunton Yeovil

South Yorkshire	Suffolk	Surrey	Tyne & Wear	Warwickshire	West Midlands	
Sheffield	Bury St. Edmunds Ipswich Lowestoft	Guildford Staines	Newcastle Sunderland	Stratford-upon-Avon	Birmingham Coventry Dudley	Redditch Solihull Stoke	Sutton Coldfield Wolverhampton

West Sussex		West Yorkshire		Wiltshire	
Crawley	Worthing	Bradford	Leeds	Salisbury	Swindon

Wales

Clwyd	Dyfed		Gwent	Gwynedd	Mid Glamorgan	Powys
Rhyl	Aberystwyth	Haverfordwest	Newport	Bangor	Merthyr Tydfil	Builth Wells

South Glamorgan	West Glamorgan			
Cardiff	Swansea	Your address details may be used to send you information about learning to drive, road safety and other motoring matters. Please tick the box if you do not wish to receive such information.		☐

Telephone Payment by debit / credit card

You may book tests at any of these centres by ringing us on **0645 000 666** – Welsh speakers dial 0645 700 201 – A Minicom machine for the use of candidates with hearing difficulties is available on 0645 700 301 – with your credit / debit card details, Monday to Friday, 8 a.m. to 6 p.m. We are happy to accept bookings using Access, Visa, Switch and Delta cards when presented by the card holder in person.

Postal Payment

If you prefer to pay by post, please fill in the details overleaf and send this completed form with your cheque or postal order to us at:
Driving Standards Agency, P.O. Box 444, Coventry, CV1 2ZY
Cheques and Postal Orders must be made payable to **"Driving Standards Agency"**.
Please write your DVLA Driver Licence Number on the back of the cheque or postal order.

Theory Test Centres listed by County/Scottish Region

Avon	Milsom Street	Bath
	Wine Street	Bristol
Bedfordshire	Stewart Street	Luton
Berkshire	So'ton Row, Cheapside	Reading
	Hatfield Road	Slough
Borders	Market Street	Galashiels
Buckinghamshire	Elder Gate	Milton Keynes
Cambridgeshire	St Andrews Street	Cambridge
	Priestgate	Peterborough
Central	Melville Terrace	Stirling
Cheshire	Watergate Street	Chester
	High Street	Runcorn
Cleveland	Albert Road	Middlesbrough
Clwyd	to follow	Rhyl
Cornwall	Market Jew Street	Penzance
	Lemon Street	Truro
Cumbria	Duke Street	Barrow
	St Marys Gate	Carlisle
	to follow	Workington
Derbyshire	Falcon Yard	Chesterfield
	Gower Street	Derby
Devon	Queen Street	Barnstaple
	Mary Arches Street	Exeter
	Armada Way	Plymouth
	Victoria Parade	Torquay
Dorset	Old Church Road	Bournemouth
	St Mary Street	Weymouth
Dumfries & Galloway	Queensbury Square	Dumfries
	Bellavilla Road	Stranraer
County Durham	North Road	Durham
Dyfed	Pier Street	Aberystwyth
	Swan Square	Haverfordwest
East Sussex	Duke Street	Brighton
	South Street	Eastbourne
	Claremont	Hastings

Essex	Eastgate Business Ctr	Basildon
	to follow	Chelmsford
	North Station Road	Colchester
	The High	Harlow
	London Road	Southend-on-Sea
Fife	New Row	Dunfermline
Gloucestershire	North Place	Cheltenham
	Southgate Street	Gloucester
Grampian	Market Street	Aberdeen
	Maisondieu Road	Elgin
	OCCASIONAL CENTRE DUE	Huntly
Greater London	Station Rd., Sidcup	Bexley
	George Street	Croydon
	High Street	Hillingdon
	Ilford Hill	Ilford
	Penrhyn Road	Kingston
	High Road	Wood Green
	Albert Embankment	Vauxhall
Greater Manchester	London Road	Manchester
	Barn Street	Oldham
	Waterfront Quays	Salford
	Wellington Rd South	Stockport
	to follow	Wigan
Gwent	Clarence Place	Newport
Gwynedd	to follow	Bangor
Hampshire	Station Road	Aldershot
	St Johns Walk	Basingstoke
	Maytree Road	Fareham
	Hampshire Terrace	Portsmouth
	High Street	Southampton
Hereford & Worcester	Broad Street	Hereford
	Kingfisher Centre	Redditch
	Broad Street	Worcester
Hertfordshire	St Georges Way	Stevenage
	High Street	Watford
Highland	Fassifern Road	Fort William
	Academy Street	Inverness
	Somerled Square	Portree
	Argyle Street	Ullapool
	Market Square	Wick

OCCASIONAL CENTRES DUE

		Helmsdale
		Kyle of Lochalsh
		Gairloch
Humberside	Church Lane	Grimsby
	Prospect Street	Hull
	Laneham Street	Scunthorpe
Isle of Wight	to follow	Newport
Kent	Lower Bridge Street	Canterbury
	High Street	Gillingham
Lancashire	to follow	Blackpool
	Churchgate	Bolton
	Chapel Street	Preston
Leicestershire	Vaughan Way	Leicester
Lincolnshire	Market Place	Boston
	Wharf Road	Grantham
	Brayfird Wharf	Lincoln
Lothian	George Street	Edinburgh
Merseyside	Hamilton Street	Birkenhead
	Pierhead	Liverpool
	Claughton Street	St Helens
Mid Glamorgan	Castle Street	Merthyr Tydfil
Norfolk	to follow	King's Lynn
	Rouen Road	Norwich
Northumbria	to follow	Berwick upon Tweed
	to follow	Morpeth
Northamptonshire	Derngate	Northampton
Nottinghamshire	Regent Street	Mansfield
	Friar Lane	Nottingham
Orkney	Junction Road	Kirkwall
Oxfordshire	Westgate Shopping Centre	Oxford
Powys	High Street	Builth Wells
Shetlands	Alexandra Buildings	Lerwick
Shropshire	St Mary's Court	Shrewsbury
Somerset	Bridge Street	Taunton
	Hendford	Yeovil
South Glamorgan	Queen Street	Cardiff
Strathclyde	Killoch Place	Ayr
	Kilbowie Road	Clydebank
	Ingram Street	Glasgow
	Duff Street	Greenock

	Merry Street	Motherwell
	Kintyre Place	Tarbert
	OCCASIONAL CENTRES DUE	Tobermory
		Arran
		Oban
		Islay
Suffolk	Lower Baxter Street	Bury St Edmunds
	Old Foundry Road	Ipswich
	Regent Street	Lowestoft
Surrey	High Street	Guildford
	High Street	Staines
Tayside	Nethergate Centre	Tayside
	Atholl Road	Pitlochry
Tyne & Wear	to follow	Newcastle
	Low Street	Sunderland
Warwickshire	Station Square	Coventry
	Birmingham Road	Stratford-upon-Avon
West Glamorgan	St Helens Road	Swansea
West Midlands	Gt. Charles Street	Birmingham
	Kings House	Dudley
	The Courtyard	Solihull
	Stoke Road	Stoke
	Trinity Place	Sutton Coldfield
	St Johns House	Wolverhampton
West Sussex	Orchard Road	Crawley
	High Street	Worthing
Western Isles	Bells Road	Stornoway
	OCCASIONAL CENTRES DUE	Barra
		Benbecula
Wiltshire	Scots Lane	Salisbury
	Commercial Road	Swindon
Yorkshire	West Park	Harrogate
	St Nicholas Street	Scarborough
	Clifford Street	York
	Burgess Street	Sheffield
	Chapel Street	Bradford
	The Headrow	Leeds

Occasional centres' opening frequency will depend upon local demand.